party time

Published in 2008 by Murdoch Books Pty Limited.
www.murdochbooks.com.au

Murdoch Books Australia
Pier 8/9, 23 Hickson Road
Millers Point NSW 2000
Phone: + 61 (0) 2 8220 2000
Fax: + 61 (0) 2 8220 2558

Murdoch Books UK Limited
Erico House, 6th Floor
93–99 Upper Richmond Road
Putney, London SW15 2TG
Phone: + 44 (0) 20 8785 5995
Fax: + 44 (0) 20 8785 5985

Chief Executive: Juliet Rogers
Publishing Director: Kay Scarlett

Design Manager: Vivien Valk
Concept: Sarah Odgers
Art Direction & Design: Heather Menzies
Editor: Kim Rowney
Production: Monique Layt
Photographer: Jared Fowler
Stylist: Cherise Koch
Food preparation: Alan Wilson
Introduction text: Leanne Kitchen
Recipes developed by the Murdoch Books Test Kitchen

National Library of Australia Cataloguing-in-Publication entry
Title: Party time: the party recipes you must have/series editor Jane Price.
ISBN: 978 1 92125 911 1 (pbk.)
Series: Kitchen classics
Notes: Includes index.
Subjects: Cookery. Entertaining.
Other Authors/Contributors: Price, Jane (Jane Paula Wynn)
Dewey Number: 641.568

A catalogue record for this book is available from the British Library

Colour reproduction by Splitting Image Colour Studio, Melbourne, Australia.
Printed by 1010 Printing International Ltd. in 2008. PRINTED IN CHINA.

IMPORTANT: Those who might be at risk from the effects of salmonella poisoning (the elderly, pregnant women, young children and those suffering from immune deficiency diseases) should consult their doctor with any concerns about eating raw eggs.

CONVERSION GUIDE: You may find cooking times vary depending on the oven you are using. For fan-forced ovens, as a general rule, set the oven temperature to 20°C (35°F) lower than indicated in the recipe.

party time

THE PARTY RECIPES YOU MUST HAVE

SERIES EDITOR JANE PRICE

MURDOCH BOOKS

CONTENTS

IT'S TIME TO CELEBRATE

What's not to love about a party? At a party everyone's in a good mood, everyone's on their best behaviour (hopefully) and, it goes without saying, there's a ton to eat and drink. There are myriad reasons for throwing a party. Birthdays, christenings, anniversaries and other special occasions all warrant a celebration but, of course, there are times when it's lovely to have a party for no other reason than to gather friends and family together and enjoy good food, great drinks, music and conversation. If the festivities are at your place, you'll need a good strategy to keep everyone well fed for the duration. The first decision to make when planning a party is how you intend to serve the food. Will you provide small, elegant bites that get passed around among your guests to eat out of hand? A selection of cocktail fare, such as Thai chicken cakes, rice paper rolls or cucumber and salmon bites, is the perfect choice here. Or, will people graze from a table laden with more substantial dishes, designed to be consumed from plates with a fork? Then lay out piles of lamb satays, barbecued haloumi and quail, heaps of bread, and bowls brimming with crunchy salads (wild and brown rice, and citrus and walnut, for example) and you're there. Or perhaps consider giving your party a particular cuisine theme such as Japanese (mixed tempura, California rolls, stuffed shiitake mushrooms and the like will go down an absolute treat), Spanish (with a sumptuous tapas spread) or Italian, by serving a selection of super-tasty antipasti offerings.

In *Party Time*, you'll find recipes for any and every type of party imaginable, including recipes for classic drinks such as pina colada, brandy Alexander and bloody Mary. Desserts haven't been forgotten either, because what self-respecting party doesn't end on a memorable note? Top yours off with a lavish peaches and cream trifle, some berry meringue stacks or a timeless devil's food cake and your guests will never want to leave. Which, after all, is the sign of a very successful party!

COCKTAIL HOUR

VIETNAMESE FRESH PRAWN ROLLS

100 g (3½ oz) dried mung bean vermicelli (cellophane noodles)
1 kg (2 lb 4 oz) cooked large prawns (shrimp)
20-25 rice paper wrappers, about 16 cm (6¼ inches) diameter
40 mint leaves
10 garlic chives, halved

DIPPING SAUCE
2 tablespoons satay sauce
60 ml (2 fl oz/¼ cup) hoisin sauce
1 red chilli, finely chopped
1 tablespoon chopped toasted unsalted peanuts
1 tablespoon lemon juice

MAKES ABOUT 20

Soak the noodles for 5 minutes in a small bowl with enough hot water to cover. Drain well and use scissors to roughly chop the noodles into shorter lengths.

Peel the prawns and gently pull out the dark vein from each back, starting at the head end. Cut the prawns in half horizontally.

Dip one rice paper wrapper at a time in warm water for a few seconds until softened. Drain, then place on a flat work surface. Be careful as the wrappers can tear easily when softened (we've allowed a few extra just in case).

Spoon about 1 tablespoon of noodles along the bottom third of the wrapper, leaving enough space at the sides to fold the wrapper over. Top with 2 mint leaves and 2 prawn halves. Fold in the sides towards each other and firmly roll up the wrapper, adding a garlic chive and positioning it so it points out of one end. Place the prawn roll, seam side down, on a serving plate. Cover with a damp cloth to prevent it drying out. Repeat with the remaining wrappers and ingredients.

To make the dipping sauce, combine the satay sauce, hoisin sauce, chilli, peanuts and lemon juice in a small bowl. Serve with the prawn rolls.

PREPARATION TIME: 45 MINUTES   COOKING TIME: NIL

MUSSELS WITH CRISPY PROSCIUTTO

1 tablespoon oil
1 onion, finely chopped
6 prosciutto slices, chopped
4 garlic cloves, crushed
1.5 kg (3 lb 5 oz) black mussels
60 g (2¼ oz) parmesan cheese, grated
60 g (2¼ oz) cheddar cheese, grated

MAKES ABOUT 20

Heat the oil in a small frying pan and add the onion, prosciutto and garlic. Cook over medium heat for 5–8 minutes, until the prosciutto is crispy and the onion is softened, then set aside.

Scrub the mussels with a stiff brush and pull out the hairy beards. Discard any broken mussels, or open ones that don't close when tapped on the work surface. Rinse well. Add to a large saucepan of boiling water and cook for 5 minutes, stirring occasionally. Discard any mussels that don't open. Remove the mussels from their shells, keeping half of each shell. Place 2 mussels on each half-shell and top each with a little of the prosciutto mixture.

Combine the parmesan and cheddar cheeses and sprinkle over the prosciutto mixture. Cook under a preheated grill (broiler) until the cheese has melted and the mussels are warmed through.

PREPARATION TIME: 20 MINUTES   COOKING TIME: 20 MINUTES

LAOTIAN FISH BALLS

500 g (1 lb 2 oz) firm white fish fillets
2 tablespoons fish sauce
3 red chillies, seeded and finely chopped
1½ teaspoons finely chopped lemon grass, white part only
4 garlic cloves, crushed
3 spring onions (scallions), finely chopped
4 tablespoons chopped coriander (cilantro) leaves
1 egg, beaten
2 tablespoons rice flour
oil, for deep-frying
1 lemon, cut into wedges, to serve

MAKES 24 BALLS

Finely chop the fish fillets. Alternatively, chop the fish in a food processor but be careful not to overwork it or the fish will be tough. Combine the fish and fish sauce in a bowl. Add the chilli, lemon grass, garlic, spring onion and half the coriander and mix well. Add the egg and rice flour and mix until thoroughly combined.

With slightly damp hands, make small balls from the mixture, each with a diameter of approximately 3 cm (1¼ inches).

Fill a deep heavy-based saucepan or deep-fryer one-third full of oil and heat to 180°C (350°F), or until a cube of bread dropped into the oil turns golden brown in 15 seconds. Add the fish balls in two batches and cook until golden. Drain on paper towel. Sprinkle the remaining coriander over the fish balls and serve immediately with lemon wedges.

PREPARATION TIME: 30 MINUTES   COOKING TIME: 10 MINUTES

MUSHROOMS IN BASIL PESTO ON SOURDOUGH

BASIL PESTO
25 g (³/₄ oz) basil leaves
30 g (1 oz/¹/₃ cup) grated parmesan
cheese
2 tablespoons pine nuts, toasted
2 tablespoons olive oil

1 small garlic clove, crushed
2¹/₂ tablespoons olive oil
1 sourdough bread stick, cut into
twenty-four 1 cm (¹/₂ inch)
thick slices
500 g (1 lb 2 oz) small flat mushrooms,
thinly sliced
3 teaspoons balsamic vinegar
80 g (2³/₄ oz) prosciutto slices

MAKES 24

To make the basil pesto, finely chop the basil, parmesan and pine nuts in a food processor. With the motor running, gradually add the olive oil in a thin stream and process until smooth. Season with salt and pepper.

Combine the garlic with 2 tablespoons of the olive oil in a small bowl and brush it over both sides of the bread slices. Place on baking trays and cook both sides under a preheated grill (broiler) until golden brown.

Preheat the oven to 200°C (400°F/Gas 6). Heat the remaining olive oil in a large frying pan. Add the mushrooms and cook over medium heat for 3–4 minutes, or until the mushrooms are heated through. Drain away any liquid. Add the pesto and vinegar to the mushrooms, stir to combine, then cook over low heat for 1–2 minutes to heat through.

To assemble, top the toasts with the pesto mushrooms, then torn and folded prosciutto. Place on baking trays and bake for 6 minutes, or until the prosciutto is crisp. Serve immediately.

PREPARATION TIME: 20 MINUTES   COOKING TIME: 20 MINUTES

NOTE: The basil pesto can be made up to 3 days ahead of time. Cover and refrigerate.

BREADED SCAMPI

1 kg (2 lb 4 oz) peeled raw scampi or peeled raw large prawns (shrimp)
60 g (2¼ oz/½ cup) plain (all-purpose) flour
4 eggs, lightly beaten
200 g (7 oz/2 cups) dry breadcrumbs
1 tablespoon finely chopped flat-leaf (Italian) parsley
oil, for deep-frying
tartare sauce, to serve
lemon wedges, to serve

SERVES 4

Pat the scampi dry with paper towel, then toss them in the flour and shake off any excess. Dip into the egg, then the combined breadcrumbs and parsley.

Fill a deep heavy-based saucepan or deep-fryer one-third full of oil and heat to 180°C (350°F), or until a cube of bread dropped into the oil turns golden brown in 15 seconds. Deep-fry the scampi in batches for 2 minutes, or until golden and cooked through. Drain on paper towel. Serve with tartare sauce and lemon wedges.

PREPARATION TIME: 20 MINUTES   COOKING TIME: 10 MINUTES

CRUMBED CALAMARI WITH CHILLI PLUM SAUCE

500 g (1 lb 2 oz) squid hoods
30 g (1 oz/¼ cup) plain (all-purpose) flour, seasoned
1 egg, lightly beaten
240 g (8½ oz/3 cups) fresh breadcrumbs
oil, for deep-frying

CHILLI PLUM SAUCE
1 teaspoon oil
1 garlic clove, crushed
310 g (11 oz/1 cup) dark plum jam
80 ml (2½ fl oz/⅓ cup) white vinegar
1–2 tablespoons sweet chilli sauce

SERVES 4

Pat the squid dry with paper towels. Remove the quill and any skin. Cut into 1 cm (½ inch) rings and set aside.

To make the chilli plum sauce, heat the oil in a small saucepan over low heat and cook the garlic until softened. Increase the heat to medium, stir in the jam, vinegar and sweet chilli sauce until combined. Set aside.

Put the seasoned flour in a plastic bag, add the squid rings and toss. Dip each ring in beaten egg, drain off the excess, then coat in breadcrumbs. Pat the crumbs lightly onto the rings and shake off any excess crumbs.

Fill a deep heavy-based saucepan or deep-fryer one-third full of oil and heat to 180°C (350°F), or until a cube of bread dropped into the oil turns golden brown in 15 seconds. Cook the squid rings in batches for 3 minutes, or until golden. Drain on crumpled paper towel and keep warm. Skim the crumbs from the surface of the oil between batches. Serve hot with the chilli plum sauce.

PREPARATION TIME: 25 MINUTES   COOKING TIME: 15 MINUTES

CRISPY SKIN CHICKEN

1.3 kg (3 lb) chicken
1 tablespoon honey
1 star anise
1 strip dried mandarin or tangerine peel
oil, for deep-frying
spring onions (scallions), thinly sliced
diagonally, to garnish
2 lemons, cut into wedges

FIVE-SPICE SALT
2 tablespoons salt
1 teaspoon white peppercorns
1/2 teaspoon Chinese five-spice
1/2 teaspoon ground white pepper

SERVES 4

Wash the chicken in cold water. Put the chicken in a large saucepan and cover with cold water. Add the honey, star anise, mandarin peel and 1 teaspoon salt and bring to the boil. Reduce the heat to low and simmer for 15 minutes. Turn off the heat and leave the chicken, covered, for a further 15 minutes. Transfer the chicken to a plate to cool.

Cut the chicken in half lengthways. Place it on paper towel, uncovered, in the refrigerator for 20 minutes.

Fill a wok or deep heavy-based saucepan one-third full of oil and heat to 160°C (315°F), or until a cube of bread dropped into the oil turns golden brown in 30–35 seconds. Very gently lower in half of the chicken, skin side down. Cook for 6 minutes, then carefully turn the chicken over and cook for another 6 minutes, making sure all the skin comes in contact with the oil. Drain on paper towel. Repeat with the second chicken half.

To make the five-spice salt, put the salt and peppercorns in a small frying pan and dry-fry until the mixture smells fragrant and the salt is slightly browned. Crush the mixture using a mortar and pestle or wrap in foil and crush it with a rolling pin. Mix with the Chinese five-spice and white pepper and place in a small, shallow dish.

Use a cleaver or a large kitchen knife to chop the chicken halves into smaller pieces. Sprinkle over the five-spice salt and garnish with spring onion. Serve with lemon wedges.

PREPARATION TIME: 20 MINUTES +   COOKING TIME: 40 MINUTES

NOTE: Any left-over five-spice salt can be stored in a dry, airtight container for several months.

TORTILLA FLUTES

60 ml (2 fl oz/¼ cup) olive oil
2 small onions, finely chopped
2 garlic cloves, crushed
½ teaspoon chilli powder
2 teaspoons ground cumin
1 kg (2 lb 4 oz) cooked chicken meat, finely chopped
2 tablespoons finely chopped coriander (cilantro) leaves
24 soft flour or corn tortillas
oil, for shallow-frying
red or green chilli sauce, to serve
1 avocado, sliced, to serve

MAKES 24

Heat the olive oil in a frying pan over medium heat and fry the onion and garlic for 2–3 minutes, or until the onion is just tender but not soft. Add the chilli powder and cumin and stir for 1 minute. Add the chicken and mix well. Cook over medium heat until just heated through. Stir in the coriander and remove from the heat.

Soften the tortillas, one at a time, by heating in a dry heavy-based frying pan over high heat for about 30 seconds each side. Lay a tortilla flat on the work surface and place a large spoonful of chicken mixture along the centre. Carefully roll up to form a flute.

Pour oil into a deep heavy-based frying pan to 5 cm (2 inches) deep and heat to 180°C (350°F), or until a cube of bread dropped into the oil turns golden brown in 15 seconds. Holding the flute together with tongs (or fasten with toothpicks), cook one at a time until slightly crisp. Drain on crumpled paper towel. Serve with chilli sauce and avocado slices.

PREPARATION TIME: 40 MINUTES   COOKING TIME: 30–40 MINUTES

GOLDEN PRAWN PUFFS

750 g (1 lb 10 oz) raw prawns (shrimp)
4 red chillies, finely chopped
1 large handful coriander (cilantro) leaves
2 egg whites
1 tablespoon finely grated fresh ginger
2 garlic cloves, chopped
1 tablespoon fish sauce
60 g (2¼ oz/⅓ cup) rice flour or cornflour (cornstarch)
125 ml (4 fl oz/½ cup) oil
chilli sauce, to serve

SERVES 4–6

Peel the prawns and gently pull out the dark vein from each prawn back, starting at the head end.

Put the prawn meat, chilli, coriander, egg whites, ginger, garlic and fish sauce in a food processor and process for 10 seconds, just until the mixture is well combined. Transfer to a bowl and stir in the flour. Refrigerate for at least 30 minutes, or until you are ready to fry the puffs.

Pour the oil into a deep heavy-based saucepan and heat to 180°C (350°F), or until a cube of bread dropped into the oil turns golden brown in 15 seconds. Very gently drop rounded teaspoons of the prawn mixture into the hot oil and cook for 2 minutes, carefully turning them with tongs until golden brown on all sides. Drain on paper towel and serve with the chilli sauce.

PREPARATION TIME: 20 MINUTES +   COOKING TIME: 10–15 MINUTES

SCALLOPS AND VEGETABLES WITH BALSAMIC DRESSING

BALSAMIC DRESSING
80 ml (2$\frac{1}{2}$ fl oz/$\frac{1}{3}$ cup) olive oil
1 tablespoon balsamic vinegar
$\frac{1}{2}$ teaspoon dijon mustard
$\frac{1}{2}$ teaspoon honey

16 large scallops, in their shells
olive oil, for brushing
1 tablespoon olive oil
2 spring onions (scallions), finely chopped
2 bacon slices, finely chopped
$\frac{1}{2}$ small red capsicum (pepper), seeded and finely diced
$\frac{1}{2}$ celery stalk, finely diced
1 tablespoon finely chopped flat-leaf (Italian) parsley
100 g (3$\frac{1}{2}$ oz) mixed salad leaves
60 g (2$\frac{1}{4}$ oz) snow pea (mangetout) sprouts, trimmed
1 spring onion (scallion), extra, shredded, to garnish

SERVES 4

To make the balsamic dressing, combine the olive oil, vinegar, mustard and honey in a jar and shake well. Set aside.

Slice or pull off any vein, membrane or hard white muscle from the scallops, leaving any roe attached. Gently pat dry with paper towel. Very lightly brush the scallops with olive oil and place on a large baking tray in their shells. Preheat the grill (broiler) to hot.

Heat the olive oil in a heavy-based frying pan. Add the chopped spring onion and bacon and cook for 2 minutes. Add the capsicum and celery and cook for 3 minutes, stirring frequently, until the vegetables are softened. Add the parsley and season well with salt and pepper.

Put the scallops on the tray under the hot grill and cook for 1–2 minutes, taking care not to overcook them. Remove from the tray and arrange the shells around the outside of a platter. Spoon some warm vegetable mixture over each scallop. Arrange the salad leaves and snow pea sprouts in the centre and garnish with the shredded spring onion. Drizzle a little balsamic dressing over the scallops and the salad before serving.

PREPARATION TIME: 30 MINUTES   COOKING TIME: 7 MINUTES

HONEY GARLIC RIBS

1.5 kg (3 lb 5 oz) American-style pork
spare ribs
175 g (6 oz/½ cup) honey
6 garlic cloves, crushed
5 cm (2 inch) piece fresh ginger,
finely grated
¼ teaspoon Tabasco sauce
60 ml (2 fl oz/¼ cup) chilli sauce
2 teaspoons grated orange zest

MAKES ABOUT 30

Cut the ribs into small pieces, with one or two bones per piece. Put the ribs in a large dish. Combine the remaining ingredients and pour over the ribs. Stir until well coated. Refrigerate for several hours, or overnight.

Preheat the oven to 200°C (400°F/Gas 6). Drain the ribs and place the marinade in a small saucepan. Put the ribs in one or two large shallow roasting tins in a single layer. Bring the marinade to the boil and simmer gently for 3–4 minutes, or until it has thickened and reduced slightly.

Brush the ribs with the marinade and bake for 50 minutes, basting with the marinade three or four times. Cook until the ribs are well browned and tender. Serve hot with any remaining marinade.

PREPARATION TIME: 20 MINUTES +   COOKING TIME: 55 MINUTES

PRAWN, CORN AND SWEET CHILLI DIP

1 kg (2 lb 4 oz) cooked medium prawns
(shrimp)
60 ml (2 fl oz/¼ cup) lime juice
110 g (3¾ oz/¾ cup) frozen corn
kernels
3 teaspoons finely grated lime zest
250 g (9 oz) cream cheese, softened
3 tablespoons finely snipped chives
1 tablespoon sweet chilli sauce
4 cooked large prawns (shrimp),
to garnish

SERVES 8

Peel the medium prawns and gently pull out the dark vein from each prawn back, starting at the head end. Pat dry with paper towel and put in a non-metallic bowl. Stir in the lime juice, then cover and refrigerate for 10 minutes.

Cook the corn kernels in boiling water for 5 minutes, or until tender. Drain well and pat dry with paper towel.

Process the prawns and lime juice in a food processor in short bursts for 2–3 seconds, until the prawns are finely chopped but not minced (ground). Transfer to a bowl and stir in the corn, lime zest, cream cheese and chives. Add the sweet chilli sauce and mix well. Cover with plastic wrap and refrigerate for at least 2 hours.

Just before serving, peel and devein the large prawns, leaving the tails intact. Transfer the dip to a serving bowl and garnish with the peeled prawns. Serve with Melba toast or pitta bread, for dipping.

PREPARATION TIME: 40 MINUTES +   COOKING TIME: 5 MINUTES

CHILLI CRAB AND TOMATO DIP

1 small ripe tomato
350 g (12 oz) tinned crabmeat, drained
200 g (7 oz) neufchâtel cheese, softened
(see Note)
2 tablespoons chilli sauce
2 teaspoons tomato paste
(concentrated purée)
1 teaspoon finely grated lemon zest
2 teaspoons lemon juice
1 small onion, finely grated
2 spring onions (scallions), finely sliced

SERVES 6

Score a cross in the base of the tomato. Place in a heatproof bowl and cover with boiling water. Leave for 30 seconds, transfer to cold water, then drain and peel the skin away from the cross. Cut the tomato in half, scoop out the seeds with a teaspoon and finely chop the flesh.

Squeeze any liquid from the crabmeat with your hands. Beat the cheese in a bowl with a wooden spoon until smooth, then stir in the crabmeat, chilli sauce, tomato paste, lemon zest, lemon juice and grated onion. Season well with salt and pepper and spoon into a serving bowl.

Scatter the spring onion and tomato over the top. Refrigerate, covered, before serving. Serve the dip with lightly toasted bread if desired.

PREPARATION TIME: 25 MINUTES   COOKING TIME: NIL

NOTE: Neufchâtel is a smooth, mild, good-quality cream cheese available from delicatessens. If it is not available, another cream cheese can be used instead.

SUGAR CANE PRAWNS

1 kg (2 lb 4 oz) raw prawns (shrimp)
2 tablespoons chopped coriander
(cilantro) leaves
2 tablespoons chopped mint
1 lemon grass stem, white part only,
finely chopped
1 small red chilli, seeded and chopped
1 garlic clove, crushed
1½ tablespoons fish sauce
2 teaspoons lime juice
½ teaspoon sugar
10 pieces sugar cane, each
10 cm (4 inches) long and
5 mm (¼ inch) wide
lime wedges, to serve

MAKES 10

Peel the prawns and gently pull out the dark vein from each prawn back, starting at the head end. Roughly chop the prawns. Put the prawns, ¼ teaspoon salt and the remaining ingredients (except the sugar cane and lime wedges) in a food processor and process until smooth.

With slightly damp hands, roll 2 tablespoons of the prawn mixture into a ball, then mould around the middle of a sugar cane skewer, pressing firmly to secure onto the skewer. Repeat with the remaining mixture and sugar cane. Refrigerate the skewers for 15 minutes.

Line a bamboo steamer with baking paper and, working in batches, put the skewers in a single layer in the steamer. Cover and steam over a wok of simmering water for 7–8 minutes, or until cooked through.

Serve the skewers with lime wedges or with a dipping sauce made up of sweet chilli sauce mixed with a little fish sauce.

PREPARATION TIME: 30 MINUTES +   COOKING TIME: 15 MINUTES

GLAZED CHICKEN WINGS

2 kg (4 lb 8 oz) chicken wings
125 ml (4 fl oz/½ cup) barbecue sauce
160 g (5½ oz/½ cup) apricot jam
2 tablespoons white vinegar
2 tablespoons soy sauce
2 tablespoons tomato sauce (ketchup)
1 tablespoon sesame oil
2 garlic cloves, crushed

MAKES ABOUT 40

Trim the excess fat from the chicken wings and put in a large bowl.

Put the barbecue sauce, jam, vinegar, soy sauce, tomato sauce, sesame oil and garlic in a small saucepan over low heat and stir until just combined. Cool slightly, pour over the chicken wings and mix well. Cover and marinate in the refrigerator for at least 2 hours.

Preheat the oven to 180°C (350°F/Gas 4). Drain the excess marinade from the wings and reserve. Put the wings in a lightly greased roasting tin and bake for 45 minutes, or until the chicken is cooked through, turning halfway through cooking time. Brush the wings occasionally with the reserved marinade. To prevent sticking, add a little water to the tin. Serve hot with plenty of paper napkins.

PREPARATION TIME: 30 MINUTES +   COOKING TIME: 45 MINUTES

THAI BEEF SALAD
RICE PAPER ROLLS

DIPPING SAUCE
60 ml (2 fl oz/¼ cup) soy sauce
1 tablespoon rice vinegar
1 teaspoon sesame oil
1 tablespoon mirin
2 teaspoons finely julienned fresh ginger

80 ml (2½ fl oz/⅓ cup) kecap manis
(see Notes)
80 ml (2½ fl oz/⅓ cup) lime juice
1 tablespoon sesame oil
2 small red chillies, finely chopped
300 g (10½ oz) beef eye fillet
1 lemon grass stem, white part only,
finely chopped
3 tablespoons finely chopped mint
3 tablespoons finely chopped coriander
(cilantro) leaves
1½ tablespoons fish sauce
60 ml (2 fl oz/¼ cup) lime juice, extra
16 square (16 cm/6¼ inch) rice paper
wrappers (see Notes)

MAKES 16

To make the dipping sauce, combine the ingredients in a small bowl. Set aside until ready to serve.

Mix the kecap manis, lime juice, sesame oil and half the chilli in a large non-metallic bowl. Add the beef and toss well to ensure the beef is well coated in the marinade. Cover with plastic wrap and refrigerate for 2 hours.

Heat a chargrill pan or barbecue grill over high heat and cook the beef for 2–3 minutes on each side, or until cooked to your liking. The beef should be cooked just until it is still pink in the middle so that it remains tender. Cool, then slice into thin strips, against the grain.

Combine the beef with the lemon grass, mint, coriander, fish sauce, extra lime juice and remaining chilli, then toss well.

Dip one rice paper wrapper at a time in warm water for a few seconds until softened. Drain, then place on a flat surface. Put a tablespoon of the mixture in the centre of the rice paper wrapper and roll up, tucking in the sides. Repeat with the remaining ingredients to make 16 rolls in total. Serve with the dipping sauce.

PREPARATION TIME: 35 MINUTES +   COOKING TIME: 5 MINUTES

NOTES: Kecap manis is also known as sweet soy sauce. It is a thick dark sauce used in Indonesian cooking as a seasoning and condiment. If it is not available, use soy sauce mixed with a little soft brown sugar.
    If square rice paper wrappers are not available, use round wrappers.

CUCUMBER AND SALMON BITES

250 g (9 oz) cream cheese or neufchâtel cheese, softened
210 g (7$\frac{1}{2}$ oz) tinned red or pink salmon, drained
1 tablespoon sour cream
1 tablespoon mayonnaise
1 tablespoon finely chopped coriander (cilantro) leaves
1 tablespoon finely snipped chives
2 teaspoons finely chopped lemon thyme
1–2 teaspoons lemon juice
4 Lebanese (short) cucumbers, thickly sliced
dill sprigs, to garnish

MAKES ABOUT 40

Beat the cream cheese in a small bowl with electric beaters until soft and creamy. Add the salmon, sour cream, mayonnaise, coriander, chives and lemon thyme. Add the lemon juice, to taste, and season with salt and pepper. Beat for 1 minute, or until combined.

Place a teaspoon of the cheese mixture on each cucumber round and garnish with the dill.

PREPARATION TIME: 20 MINUTES   COOKING TIME: NIL

NOTE: The salmon mixture can be prepared a day ahead and refrigerated in an airtight container. Slice the cucumber into rounds and assemble just before serving.

CARAMELISED APPLE ON PUMPERNICKEL

2 golden delicious or pink lady apples (see Note)
2 tablespoons lemon juice
60 g (2$\frac{1}{4}$ oz/$\frac{1}{2}$ cup) icing (confectioners') sugar
30 g (1 oz) unsalted butter
175 g (6 oz) blue cheese, crumbled
30 g (1 oz) walnuts, finely chopped
1 celery stalk, finely chopped
250 g (9 oz) pumpernickel rounds

MAKES ABOUT 24

Peel and core the apples and slice each into twelve wedges. Brush with lemon juice and sprinkle generously with icing sugar.

Heat the butter in a frying pan and, when foaming, add a few apple wedges. Cook until brown and beginning to caramelise. Remove from the pan and cool on a piece of baking paper. Repeat with the remaining apple, adding more butter to the pan as needed.

Combine the blue cheese, walnuts and celery in a bowl and spoon a little onto each pumpernickel round. Top with a caramelised apple.

PREPARATION TIME: 30 MINUTES   COOKING TIME: 15 MINUTES

NOTE: Granny smith apples are not suitable for this recipe.

Cucumber and salmon bites

THAI CHICKEN CAKES

4 eggs, lightly beaten
2 tablespoons finely chopped coriander (cilantro) leaves
1 tablespoon fish sauce
2 tablespoons oil
500 g (1 lb 2 oz) minced (ground) chicken
3 lemon grass stems, white part only, finely chopped
2 garlic cloves, crushed
4 spring onions (scallions), chopped
60 ml (2 fl oz/¼ cup) lime juice
2 large handfuls coriander (cilantro) leaves and stems
2 tablespoons sweet chilli sauce
1 tablespoon fish sauce
1 egg, extra, lightly beaten
125 ml (4 fl oz/½ cup) coconut milk
6 red chillies, seeded and very thinly sliced, to garnish

MAKES 36

Preheat the oven to 200°C (400°F/Gas 6). Lightly grease three 12-hole mini muffin tins.

Combine the eggs, finely chopped coriander and fish sauce in a bowl. Heat the oil in a 25–28 cm (10–11¼ inch) frying pan and pour in the egg mixture. Cook over medium heat for about 2 minutes each side, or until golden. Roll up the omelette and shred finely. Set aside.

Put the chicken, lemon grass, garlic, spring onion, lime juice, coriander leaves and stems, sweet chilli sauce, fish sauce, extra egg and coconut milk in a food processor. Process until the mixture is fine but not smooth. Spoon into the prepared tins and top with a little shredded omelette.

Bake for 15 minutes, or until cooked through. Rotate the tins once during cooking time to ensure the chicken cakes all cook through. Serve hot, garnished with the chilli.

PREPARATION TIME: 20 MINUTES   COOKING TIME: 20 MINUTES

PORK AND LETTUCE PARCELS

500 g (1 lb 2 oz) pork loin
5 cm (2 inch) piece fresh ginger,
thinly sliced
1 tablespoon fish sauce
20 thin spring onions (scallions)
2 soft-leaf lettuces, such as butter lettuce
1 Lebanese (short) cucumber, thinly sliced
3 tablespoons mint
3 tablespoons coriander (cilantro) leaves
2 green chillies, seeded and very
thinly sliced (optional)
2 teaspoons caster (superfine) sugar

LEMON AND GARLIC DIPPING SAUCE
60 ml (2 fl oz/¼ cup) lemon juice
2 tablespoons fish sauce
1 tablespoon caster (superfine) sugar
2 small red chillies, chopped
3 garlic cloves, finely chopped

SERVES 4–6

Put the pork, ginger and fish sauce in a large saucepan and cover with cold water. Bring to the boil, then reduce the heat and simmer, covered, for about 45 minutes, or until the pork is tender. Remove the pork and allow to cool. Discard the liquid.

Trim both ends from the spring onions so you have long stems of equal length. Bring a large saucepan of water to the boil and blanch the spring onions, two or three at a time, for about 2 minutes, until softened. Remove the spring onions from the hot water with tongs and place in a bowl of iced water. Drain and lay them flat and straight on a tray.

Separate the lettuce into leaves. If the leaves have a firm section at the base, trim this away (or making a neat parcel will be difficult).

When the pork is cool enough to handle, cut it into thin slices and finely shred each slice. Spread out a lettuce leaf and place about 1 tablespoon of the shredded pork in the centre of the leaf. Top with a few slices of cucumber, a few mint and coriander leaves, a little green chilli if using, and a light sprinkling of sugar. Fold a section of the lettuce over the filling, bring in the sides to meet each other, and carefully roll up the parcel. Tie one of the spring onions around the parcel, trim off the excess or tie it into a bow. Repeat with the remaining ingredients.

To make the lemon and garlic dipping sauce, combine the lemon juice, fish sauce, sugar, chilli and garlic in a bowl, stirring until the sugar has dissolved. Arrange the pork and lettuce parcels on a serving platter and serve with the dipping sauce.

PREPARATION TIME: 1 HOUR   COOKING TIME: 1 HOUR

GRILLED RICE WITH DIPPING SAUCE

DIPPING SAUCE
125 ml (4 fl oz/$^{1}/_{2}$ cup) rice vinegar
110 g (3$^{3}/_{4}$ oz/$^{1}/_{2}$ cup) sugar
2 garlic cloves, crushed
2 red bird's eye chillies, finely chopped

2 eggs
1 tablespoon fish sauce
$^{1}/_{2}$ teaspoon sugar
550 g (1 lb 4 oz/3 cups) cooked glutinous short-grain rice, well drained

MAKES 6

To make the dipping sauce, combine the ingredients in a small bowl and stir until the sugar is dissolved.

Soak 6 wooden skewers in water for 30 minutes to ensure they don't burn during cooking. Line a grill (broiler) tray with foil and brush it lightly with oil. Preheat the grill to its highest setting.

Beat the eggs with the fish sauce, sugar and a pinch of black pepper. Pour into a long tray, large enough to fit the skewers.

Divide the cooked rice into six portions and form each portion into three small balls. Press each ball to flatten it, then thread three flat rice rounds onto each skewer. Dip each rice skewer into the egg mixture, shake off any excess and put it on the grill tray. Grill (broil) the rice until browned on one side, then turn it over and grill the other side. Serve with the dipping sauce.

PREPARATION TIME: 30 MINUTES +   COOKING TIME: 15 MINUTES

PRAWN CUTLETS

1 kg (2 lb 4 oz) raw large prawns (shrimp)
4 eggs
2 tablespoons soy sauce
cornflour (cornstarch), to coat
200 g (7 oz/2 cups) dry breadcrumbs
oil, for deep-frying
tartare sauce, to serve
lemon wedges, to serve

SERVES 4–6

Peel the prawns, leaving the tails intact. Slit the prawns open down the backs, remove the veins and then gently flatten open with your fingers.

Beat the eggs and soy sauce in a small bowl. Coat the prawns in cornflour and shake off the excess. Dip them in the egg mixture and finally press them in the breadcrumbs. Chill for 15 minutes.

Fill a deep heavy-based saucepan or deep-fryer one-third full of oil and heat to 180°C (350°F), or until a cube of bread dropped into the oil turns golden brown in 15 seconds. Deep-fry the prawns in batches until lightly golden. Drain on crumpled paper towel, then serve with tartare sauce and lemon wedges.

PREPARATION TIME: 30 MINUTES +   COOKING TIME: 10 MINUTES

Grilled rice with dipping sauce

MUSHROOMS STUFFED WITH SCALLOPS

16 dried Chinese mushrooms
2 tablespoons mirin
2 tablespoons soy sauce
5 cm (2 inch) piece fresh ginger, chopped
16 scallops, cleaned
3 cm (1¼ inch) piece fresh ginger, extra
1 spring onion (scallion)
1 red chilli, seeded
2 teaspoons chopped lemon grass, white part only
1 tablespoon sweet sherry
1 tablespoon oyster sauce
½ teaspoon sesame oil
½ teaspoon caster (superfine) sugar

MAKES 16

Soak the dried mushrooms in boiling water for 30 minutes. Drain and put in a saucepan with 375 ml (13 fl oz/1½ cups) water, mirin, soy sauce and chopped ginger. Simmer for 20 minutes, then remove from the pan. When the mushrooms are cool, discard the stalks.

Place one scallop in the centre of each mushroom. Cut the extra piece of ginger, the spring onion and chilli into thin strips. Sprinkle over the scallops, then top with the lemon grass.

Line a bamboo steamer with baking paper and, working in two batches, put the mushrooms in a single layer in the steamer. Cover and steam over a wok of simmering water for 3-5 minutes, or until the scallops are tender.

Combine the sherry, oyster sauce, sesame oil and sugar. Drizzle over the scallops before serving.

PREPARATION TIME: 20 MINUTES +   COOKING TIME: 30 MINUTES

STEAMED GINGER MUSSELS

2 kg (4 lb 8 oz) black mussels
1 tablespoon fish sauce
2 garlic cloves, crushed
4 small red Asian shallots, thinly sliced
1 tablespoon finely shredded fresh ginger
2 red bird's eye chillies, seeded and thinly sliced
2 lemon grass stems, white part only, bruised and cut into 5 cm (2 inch) lengths
4 fresh makrut (kaffir lime) leaves
1 tablespoon lime juice
1 lime, cut into wedges

SERVES 4

Scrub the mussels with a stiff brush and pull out the hairy beards. Discard any broken mussels or open ones that don't close when tapped on the work surface. Rinse well.

Pour the fish sauce and 125 ml (4 fl oz/½ cup) water into a wok and bring to the boil. Add half the mussels and scatter with half the garlic, shallots, ginger, chilli, lemon grass and lime leaves. Cover and steam over high heat for 2-3 minutes, shaking the wok frequently, until the mussels have just opened. Remove the mussels with a slotted spoon, discarding any that have not opened. Repeat with the remaining mussels and aromatics (you do not need to add more water or fish sauce to the wok at this stage). Put the mussels in a serving bowl, leaving the cooking liquid in the wok.

Add the lime juice to the wok and season with salt and pepper. Pour the liquid and the aromatics over the mussels and serve with lime wedges.

PREPARATION TIME: 15 MINUTES   COOKING TIME: 10 MINUTES

Mushrooms stuffed with scallops

CURRIED MEATBALLS

2 tablespoons olive oil

1 large onion, finely chopped

1 garlic clove, finely chopped

45 g (1½ oz) butter

1 tablespoon curry powder

2 tablespoons plain (all-purpose) flour

185 ml (6 fl oz/¾ cup) milk

1 tablespoon tomato or mango chutney, plus extra, to serve

400 g (14 oz) minced (ground), cooked, cold lamb, beef or chicken

30 g (1 oz/¼ cup) plain (all-purpose) flour, extra, to coat

2 eggs

125 g (4½ oz/1¼ cups) dry breadcrumbs

oil, for deep-frying

MAKES 25–30

Heat the olive oil in a large saucepan over medium heat, add the onion and cook for 5 minutes, or until soft and golden. Add the garlic and cook for 30 seconds. Add the butter to the pan and, when melted, stir in the curry powder until aromatic. Add the flour and cook for 1 minute, or until foaming. Remove from the heat and gradually stir in the milk.

Return to the heat and stir constantly until the sauce boils and thickens, then reduce the heat and simmer for 2 minutes. Add the chutney and ¼ teaspoon each of salt and black pepper. Remove from the heat and add the meat, stirring until the mixture is well combined. Cool, cover with plastic wrap and refrigerate for at least 1 hour.

Using wet hands, form tablespoons of the mixture into balls and place on trays lined with baking paper.

Place the extra flour on a plate. Beat the eggs in a shallow bowl. Put the breadcrumbs on a sheet of baking paper. Lightly coat the meatballs in flour, shake off any excess, dip into the egg and then coat with crumbs. Return to the tray, then cover and refrigerate for 1 hour, or overnight.

Fill a deep heavy-based saucepan or deep-fryer one-third full of oil and heat to 180°C (350°F), or until a cube of bread dropped into the oil turns golden brown in 15 seconds. Deep-fry the meatballs in batches for about 2 minutes each batch, or until golden brown all over. Remove from the oil with a slotted spoon and drain on crumpled paper towel. Serve hot with tomato chutney.

PREPARATION TIME: 40 MINUTES +   COOKING TIME: 40 MINUTES

NOTES: You can use any left-over roast meat. Mince (grind) it in a food processor or cut finely with a sharp knife.

The meat mixture can be made up to 2 days ahead. The crumbed balls can be frozen for up to 2 months. Thaw thoroughly before frying.

COCONUT-CRUSTED LAMB CUTLETS

24 thin, lean lamb cutlets
1 large onion, grated
2 garlic cloves, crushed
2 teaspoons ground turmeric
1 tablespoon soft brown sugar or grated palm sugar (jaggery)
60 g (2^1/$_4$ oz/^{2}/$_3$ cup) desiccated coconut
2 teaspoons soy sauce
2 tablespoons lemon juice

MAKES 24

Trim the lamb cutlets of excess fat and sinew. Combine all the remaining ingredients in a non-metallic bowl with 1 teaspoon salt and ^{1}/$_2$ teaspoon pepper. Stir until the coconut is thoroughly moistened.

Add the lamb cutlets to the bowl and press the coconut mixture onto the surface of each cutlet. Cover with plastic wrap and refrigerate for 2 hours.

Preheat a grill (broiler) and lightly oil the grill tray. Working in batches if necessary, cook the cutlets for 3–5 minutes on each side, or until crisp and golden brown.

PREPARATION TIME: 10 MINUTES +   COOKING TIME: 10–20 MINUTES

STEAMED SCALLOPS

1 small red capsicum (pepper), quartered, seeds and membrane removed
90 g (3^1/$_4$ oz) butter, softened
1 tablespoon snipped chives
2 teaspoons dijon mustard
2 teaspoons lime juice
24 scallops, in their shells
6 spring onions (scallions), cut into long thin strips

SERVES 4

Put the capsicum quarters, skin side up, under a hot grill (broiler). Cook until the skin blackens and blisters. Remove from the grill and put in a plastic bag until cool, then peel off the skin. Put the capsicum flesh into a food processor and purée until smooth.

Beat the butter in a small bowl until light, then beat in the chives, mustard, lime juice and capsicum purée. Season with ^{1}/$_4$ teaspoon pepper.

Remove the scallops from their shells and slice or pull off any vein, membrane or hard white muscle from each. Place a few strips of spring onion over each shell and top with the scallop. Put the scallops in their shells in a single layer in a bamboo or metal steamer. Place over a large saucepan or wok of simmering water and steam the scallops in batches for 2–3 minutes. Transfer to a warmed serving platter while cooking the remaining scallops.

Top with a dollop of the chive and capsicum butter. The butter will melt from the heat of the scallops.

PREPARATION TIME: 20 MINUTES   COOKING TIME: 10 MINUTES

Coconut-crusted lamb cutlets

SMOKED FIVE-SPICE CHICKEN

1.7 kg (3 lb 12 oz) chicken
60 ml (2 fl oz/$1/4$ cup) soy sauce
1 tablespoon finely grated fresh ginger
2 strips dried mandarin or tangerine peel
1 star anise
$1/4$ teaspoon Chinese five-spice
3 tablespoons soft brown sugar
1 spring onion (scallion), sliced diagonally, to garnish
1 small handful coriander (cilantro) sprigs, to garnish

SERVES 6

Wash the chicken in cold water, then pat dry with paper towels. Discard any large pieces of fat from inside the chicken.

Put the chicken in a large non-metallic bowl along with the soy sauce and ginger. Cover and marinate for at least 4 hours, or leave overnight in the refrigerator, turning occasionally.

Put a small rack in the base of a saucepan large enough to hold the chicken. Add water up to the level of the rack. Place the chicken on the rack. Bring the water to the boil, cover tightly, then reduce the heat and steam for 15 minutes. Turn off the heat and allow the chicken to rest in the pan, covered, for another 15 minutes. Transfer the chicken to a bowl.

Wash the pan and line it with three or four large pieces of foil. Using a mortar and pestle, pound the dried mandarin peel and star anise until the pieces are the size of coarse breadcrumbs, or process in a food processor. Add the five-spice and brown sugar. Spread the spice mixture over the foil in the pan.

Replace the rack in the pan and place the chicken on it. Put the pan over medium heat and, when the spice mixture starts smoking, cover tightly. Reduce the heat to low and smoke the chicken for 20 minutes. Test if the chicken is cooked by piercing the thigh with a skewer; the juices should run clear. (The heat produced in this final step is very intense. When the chicken is removed from the pan, leave the pan on the stove to cool a little before handling it.)

Remove the chicken from the pan and chop it into smaller pieces using a cleaver or large kitchen knife. Transfer to a serving platter and garnish with the spring onion and coriander.

PREPARATION TIME: 30 MINUTES +   COOKING TIME: 35 MINUTES

FRIKKADELS

45 g (1½ oz/½ cup) desiccated coconut
500 g (1 lb 2 oz) minced (ground) beef
1 garlic clove, crushed
1 onion, finely chopped
1 teaspoon ground cumin
¼ teaspoon ground cinnamon
½ teaspoon finely grated lime zest
1 tablespoon chopped dill
1 egg, lightly beaten
100 g (3½ oz/1 cup) dry breadcrumbs
oil, for deep-frying

YOGHURT DIPPING SAUCE
250 g (9 oz/1 cup) plain yoghurt
1 large handful mint, finely chopped
pinch cayenne pepper

MAKES ABOUT 25

Preheat the oven to 150°C (300°F/Gas 2). Spread the coconut on a baking tray and toast it in the oven for 10 minutes, or until dark golden, shaking the tray occasionally.

Put the toasted coconut, beef, garlic, onion, cumin, cinnamon, lime zest and dill in a large bowl and mix to combine. Season with salt and pepper. Shape tablespoons of the mixture into balls. Dip the meatballs in the beaten egg and then toss to coat in the breadcrumbs.

Fill a deep heavy-based saucepan or deep-fryer one-third full of oil and heat to 180°C (350°F), or until a cube of bread dropped into the oil turns golden brown in 15 seconds. Add the meatballs in batches and cook for 5 minutes, or until deep golden brown and cooked through. Drain on paper towel.

To make the yoghurt dipping sauce, combine the ingredients in a bowl and stir to combine. Serve the frikkadels with the dipping sauce.

PREPARATION TIME: 30 MINUTES   COOKING TIME: 40 MINUTES

CRAB-STUFFED MUSHROOMS

24 small cap mushrooms
30 g (1 oz) butter, softened
4 spring onions (scallions), chopped
200 g (7 oz) tinned crabmeat, drained
2 tablespoons lemon juice
½ teaspoon chilli powder
250 g (9 oz/1 cup) sour cream
25 g (1 oz/¼ cup) grated parmesan cheese
125 g (4 oz/1 cup) grated cheddar cheese
pinch paprika

MAKES 24

Preheat the oven to 180°C (350°F/Gas 4). Remove the mushroom stalks, chop them finely and set aside. Put the mushroom caps on a baking tray.

Combine the butter, spring onion, crabmeat, lemon juice and chilli powder in a bowl. Season with pepper. Mix in the chopped mushroom stalks, sour cream and parmesan. Spoon even amounts into the mushroom caps and sprinkle with the combined cheddar and paprika.

Bake for 5–6 minutes, or until the cheese has melted and the mushrooms are heated through. Serve warm.

PREPARATION TIME: 25 MINUTES   COOKING TIME: 6 MINUTES

STRAWBERRY MARGARITA

1 egg white
salt
6 ice cubes
30 ml (1 fl oz) tequila
30 ml (1 fl oz) strawberry liqueur
30 ml (1 fl oz) lime juice cordial
30 ml (1 fl oz) lemon juice
15 ml (½ fl oz) Cointreau

MAKES 1

Frost the rim of a martini glass by lightly beating the egg white until just frothy, then dipping the rim of the martini glass first into the egg white, then into salt.

Put the ice cubes in a blender with the tequila, strawberry liqueur, lime juice cordial, lemon juice and Cointreau. Blend well, then pour into the martini glass, taking care to avoid touching the rim of the glass.

PREPARATION TIME: 5 MINUTES   COOKING TIME: NIL

BLOODY MARY

crushed ice
60 ml (2 fl oz/¼ cup) vodka
tomato juice
Tabasco sauce
worcestershire sauce
lemon juice
celery stalk, with leaves, to serve

MAKES 1

Half-fill a tall glass with crushed ice. Pour in the vodka, then top up with tomato juice and stir. Stir in a dash of Tabasco sauce, worcestershire sauce, lemon juice and a little salt and pepper. Traditionally, this drink is served with a celery stalk, including leaves, as an edible swizzle stick.

To make a virgin Mary (a non-alcoholic version), leave out the vodka.

PREPARATION TIME: 5 MINUTES   COOKING TIME: NIL

Strawberry margarita

CRANBERRY AND VODKA SPARKLE

125 ml (4 fl oz/1/2 cup) cranberry juice
125 ml (4 fl oz/1/2 cup) lemonade
or mineral water
2 teaspoons lime juice
30 ml (1 fl oz) vodka
ice cubes

MAKES 1

Combine the chilled cranberry juice and lemonade or mineral water in a jug with the lime juice, vodka and a few ice cubes. Mix well, pour into a tall glass and serve immediately.

PREPARATION TIME: 5 MINUTES   COOKING TIME: NIL

SPARKLING WINE AND BRANDY COCKTAIL

1-2 sugar cubes
Angostura bitters
15 ml (1/2 fl oz) brandy
sparkling white wine

MAKES 1

Place the sugar cubes in a champagne flute. Add a dash of Angostura bitters over the sugar, then pour in the brandy. Slowly top up the glass with chilled sparkling white wine.

PREPARATION TIME: 5 MINUTES   COOKING TIME: NIL

MANGO DAIQUIRI

6 ice cubes
45 ml (1¹/₂ fl oz) white rum
15 ml (¹/₂ fl oz) mango liqueur
30 ml (1 fl oz) lemon juice
30 ml (1 fl oz) Cointreau or
Grand Marnier
1 mango, flesh removed and
roughly chopped

MAKES 1

Combine the ice cubes in a blender with the white rum, mango liqueur, lemon juice and the Cointreau or Grand Marnier. Add the mango and blend until smooth. Pour into a large goblet-shaped glass.

PREPARATION TIME: 10 MINUTES   COOKING TIME: NIL

BUCK'S FIZZ

125 ml (4 fl oz/¹/₂ cup) fresh orange juice
Grenadine
sparkling white wine

MAKES 1

Pour the orange juice and a dash of Grenadine into a champagne flute. Slowly top up the glass with chilled sparkling white wine.

PREPARATION TIME: 5 MINUTES   COOKING TIME: NIL

Mango daiquiri

BRANDY ALEXANDER

6 ice cubes
30 ml (1 fl oz) brandy
30 ml (1 fl oz) crème de cacao
60 ml (2 fl oz/¼ cup) pouring cream
freshly grated nutmeg, to serve

MAKES 1

Put the ice cubes in a drink shaker or jug with the brandy, crème de cacao and cream. Shake or stir well, then strain into a champagne saucer and serve sprinkled lightly with some freshly grated nutmeg.

PREPARATION TIME: 5 MINUTES   COOKING TIME: NIL

PINA COLADA

6 ice cubes
45 ml (1½ fl oz) white rum
30 ml (1 fl oz) coconut cream
15 ml (½ fl oz) pouring cream
125 ml (4 fl oz/½ cup) pineapple juice
pineapple leaves, to garnish (optional)
maraschino cherry, to garnish (optional)

MAKES 1

Put the ice cubes in a drink shaker or jug with the white rum, coconut cream, cream and pineapple juice and shake or stir well. Alternatively, blend the ingredients in a blender.

Pour into a tall glass. You can garnish the glass with pineapple leaves and a maraschino cherry if you like. Serve immediately.

PREPARATION TIME: 5 MINUTES   COOKING TIME: NIL

BARBECUE BUFFET

STARS AND STRIPES BARBECUED PORK RIBS

½ teaspoon dry mustard or prepared English mustard

½ teaspoon sweet paprika

¼ teaspoon ground oregano

¼ teaspoon ground cumin

1½ tablespoons peanut oil

1 teaspoon Tabasco sauce

1 garlic clove, crushed

125 ml (4 fl oz/½ cup) tomato sauce (ketchup)

2 tablespoons tomato paste (concentrated purée)

2 tablespoons soft brown sugar

1 tablespoon worcestershire sauce

2 teaspoons brown vinegar

1.5 kg (3 lb 5 oz) American-style pork spare ribs (see Note)

MAKES ABOUT 30

To make the sauce, combine the mustard, paprika, oregano, cumin and peanut oil in a saucepan. Add the remaining ingredients, except the ribs. Cook, stirring, over medium heat for 3 minutes, or until combined. Allow to cool. Coat the ribs with the sauce, cover and marinate overnight in the refrigerator.

Heat a barbecue hotplate to hot and cook the ribs, turning frequently, until firm and well done. Cut into individual ribs before serving.

PREPARATION TIME: 30 MINUTES +   COOKING TIME: 15 MINUTES

NOTE: Buy very lean pork spare ribs as fatty ones tend to flare up and burn.

CHILLI PEPPER YABBIES

12 live yabbies or scampi

2 red chillies, seeded and chopped

125 g (4½ oz/½ cup) tomato passata (puréed tomatoes)

2 garlic cloves, crushed

6 spring onions (scallions), thinly sliced

2 tablespoons chopped basil

3 teaspoons cracked black pepper

SERVES 6

To prepare the yabbies humanely, place them in a bag in the freezer for 1 hour before you need to use them to render them unconscious. Make a small slit on the underside of each yabby tail, to allow the flesh to absorb the marinade.

To make the marinade, combine the chilli, tomato passata, garlic, spring onion, basil and cracked pepper in a large bowl and mix well. Add the yabbies, cover and refrigerate for 1 hour.

Heat a chargrill pan or barbecue hotplate and cook the yabbies, with their marinade, for 10-15 minutes, or until the flesh is just tender. Serve with a crisp green salad. Provide your guests with crab/lobster crackers (or nutcrackers) and finger bowls.

PREPARATION TIME: 15 MINUTES +   COOKING TIME: 15 MINUTES

PIRI PIRI PRAWNS

125 ml (4 fl oz/½ cup) oil

2 teaspoons chilli flakes or 1–2 red bird's eye chillies, finely chopped

4 large garlic cloves, crushed

1 kg (2 lb 4 oz) raw prawns (shrimp)

75 g (2½ oz) butter

60 ml (2 fl oz/¼ cup) lemon juice

SERVES 4

Put the oil, chilli flakes, garlic and 1 teaspoon salt in a large glass bowl and mix well.

Peel the prawns, leaving the tails intact. Gently pull the dark vein from each prawn back, starting at the head end. Stir the prawns into the chilli mixture, cover and refrigerate for 3 hours, stirring occasionally.

Heat a lightly oiled barbecue hotplate or preheat a grill (broiler) to hot. Cook the prawns for 3–5 minutes, or until tender and cooked through, brushing the prawns with the remaining oil and chilli mixture.

Meanwhile, melt the butter with the lemon juice in a small saucepan and pour into a serving jug. Serve the prawns hot, drizzled with lemon butter.

PREPARATION TIME: 20 MINUTES +   COOKING TIME: 10 MINUTES

BARBECUED SQUID

500 g (1 lb 2 oz) small squid (see Notes)

PICADA DRESSING
2 tablespoons extra virgin olive oil
2 tablespoons finely chopped
flat-leaf (Italian) parsley
1 garlic clove, crushed

SERVES 6

To prepare the squid, gently pull the tentacles away from the tubes; the intestines should come away at the same time. Cut under the eyes to remove the intestines from the tentacles, then remove the beak (if it remains in the centre of the tentacles) by using your fingers to push up the centre. Pull away the soft bone.

Rub the tubes under cold running water and the skin should come away easily. Wash the tubes and tentacles and drain well. Place in a bowl, add $\frac{1}{4}$ teaspoon salt and mix well. Cover and refrigerate for 30 minutes.

To make the picada dressing, whisk together the olive oil, parsley, garlic, some salt and $\frac{1}{4}$ teaspoon freshly ground black pepper in a small bowl.

Heat a lightly oiled barbecue hotplate or preheat a grill (broiler) to its highest setting. Cook the squid tubes in small batches for 2–3 minutes, or until they are white and tender. Cook the squid tentacles, turning to brown them all over, for 1 minute, or until they curl up. Serve hot, with the picada dressing.

PREPARATION TIME: 40 MINUTES +   COOKING TIME: 10 MINUTES

NOTES: Try to use the smallest squid you can find for this recipe. Alternatively, you can also use cuttlefish, octopus, prawns (shrimp) or even chunks of firm white fish fillet instead of the squid.
    Make the picada dressing as close to serving time as possible so the parsley doesn't discolour.

SPANISH-STYLE BEEF KEBABS

1 kg (2 lb 4 oz) rump steak
3 garlic cloves, chopped
1 tablespoon chopped flat-leaf
(Italian) parsley
80 ml (2¹/₂ fl oz/¹/₃ cup) lemon juice
lemon wedges, to serve

PAPRIKA DRESSING
2 teaspoons paprika
large pinch cayenne pepper
2 tablespoons red wine vinegar
80 ml (2¹/₂ fl oz/¹/₃ cup) olive oil

MAKES 18–20

Trim any excess fat from the beef and cut into 2 cm (³/₄ inch) pieces. Combine the beef, garlic, parsley, lemon juice and ¹/₂ teaspoon pepper in a non-metallic bowl, cover with plastic wrap and marinate in the refrigerator for 2 hours. Meanwhile, soak 18–20 wooden skewers in water for 30 minutes to ensure they don't burn during cooking.

To make the paprika dressing, whisk the paprika, cayenne pepper, vinegar, oil and ¹/₂ teaspoon salt together until well blended.

Heat a lightly oiled barbecue hotplate. Thread the pieces of marinated beef onto the skewers, then cook the kebabs, turning occasionally, for 4–5 minutes, or until cooked through. Drizzle with the paprika dressing and serve hot with lemon wedges.

PREPARATION TIME: 20 MINUTES +   COOKING TIME: 5 MINUTES

BARBECUED SALMON CUTLETS WITH CUCUMBER DRESSING

2 small Lebanese (short) cucumbers,
peeled, seeded and finely diced
1 red onion, finely chopped
1 red chilli, finely chopped
2 tablespoons pickled ginger, shredded
2 tablespoons rice wine vinegar
¹/₂ teaspoon sesame oil
4 salmon or ocean trout cutlets
1 sheet toasted nori (dried seaweed),
cut into thin strips with scissors

SERVES 4

Combine the cucumber, onion, chilli, ginger, vinegar and sesame oil in a bowl, cover and set aside at room temperature while cooking the salmon.

Heat a barbecue hotplate and lightly brush with oil. Cook the salmon for about 2 minutes on each side, or until cooked as desired. Be careful you don't overcook the fish or it will be dry — it should be just pink in the centre.

Serve the salmon topped with the cucumber dressing. Sprinkle the top with strips of toasted nori.

PREPARATION TIME: 15 MINUTES   COOKING TIME: 5 MINUTES

EGGPLANT KEBABS WITH MISO

2 eggplants (aubergines), cut into
2 cm (³/₄ inch) cubes
2 tablespoons Japanese white
sesame seeds
140 g (5 oz/¹/₂ cup) red miso paste
2 tablespoons mirin
2 tablespoons sake
60 ml (2 fl oz/¹/₄ cup) oil

MAKES 10

Soak 10 wooden skewers in water for 30 minutes to ensure they don't burn during cooking. Put the eggplant in a colander and sprinkle generously with salt. Set aside for 15 minutes, or until the moisture has been drawn out of the eggplant (this removes the bitterness). Rinse thoroughly and pat dry with paper towel.

Drain the skewers and dry with paper towel. Thread the eggplant cubes onto the skewers.

Put the sesame seeds in a dry frying pan over medium heat and toast for 3–4 minutes, shaking the pan gently, until the seeds are golden brown. Remove the seeds from the pan at once to prevent burning.

Combine the miso, mirin and sake in a small saucepan. Bring to the boil, then reduce the heat and simmer for 5 minutes.

Heat the oil on a barbecue hotplate and cook the eggplant skewers for 5 minutes, turning frequently until golden brown. Spread the miso topping over the eggplant skewers and sprinkle with the sesame seeds. Serve with rice.

PREPARATION TIME: 15 MINUTES + COOKING TIME: 15 MINUTES

BARBECUED HALOUMI

10 slices baguette
olive oil
1 garlic clove, crushed
250 g (9 oz) haloumi cheese, cut into
5 mm (¼ inch) slices
2 tablespoons chopped mint

MAKES 10

Lightly brush the bread on both sides with some olive oil. Cook on a hot barbecue hotplate on both sides until brown.

Combine a little more oil with the crushed garlic and brush over the cheese. Cook on the barbecue hotplate for 1 minute, or until soft and golden underneath. Use a spatula to remove the cheese and place some on each piece of toast. Drizzle with a little more olive oil and sprinkle with mint and some freshly ground black pepper.

PREPARATION TIME: 10 MINUTES   COOKING TIME: 8 MINUTES

BARBECUED PRAWNS
WITH ROMESCO SAUCE

30 raw large prawns (shrimp)

ROMESCO SAUCE
4 garlic cloves, unpeeled
1 roma (plum) tomato, halved and seeded
2 long red chillies
35 g (1¼ oz/¼ cup) blanched almonds
60 g (2¼ oz) sun-dried capsicums
(peppers) in oil
1 tablespoon olive oil
1 tablespoon red wine vinegar

SERVES 6–8

Peel the prawns, leaving the tails intact. Gently pull out the dark vein from each prawn back, starting at the head end. Mix with ¼ teaspoon salt and refrigerate for 30 minutes.

To make the Romesco sauce, preheat the oven to 200°C (400°F/Gas 6). Wrap the garlic cloves in foil, put on a baking tray with the tomato and chillies and bake for 12 minutes. Spread the almonds on the tray and bake for another 3–5 minutes. Leave to cool for 15 minutes.

Transfer the almonds to a small blender or food processor and blend until finely ground. Squeeze the garlic and scrape the tomato flesh into the blender, discarding the skins. Split the chillies and remove the seeds. Scrape the flesh into the blender, discarding the skins. Pat the capsicums dry with paper towel, then chop them and add to the blender with the olive oil, vinegar, some salt and 2 tablespoons water. Blend until smooth, adding more water if necessary to form a soft dipping consistency.

Brush the prawns with a little oil and cook on a hot barbecue grill for 3 minutes, or until curled up and changed in colour. Serve with the sauce.

PREPARATION TIME: 20 MINUTES +   COOKING TIME: 20 MINUTES

Barbecued haloumi

WHOLE BARBECUED FISH

750 g (1 lb 10 oz) small snapper or bream, cleaned and scaled
2 teaspoons green peppercorns
2 teaspoons chopped red chilli
3 teaspoons fish sauce
1 tablespoon oil
2 onions, thinly sliced
4 cm (1½ inch) piece fresh ginger, cut into very thin slices
3 garlic cloves, cut into very thin slices
2 teaspoons sugar
4 spring onions (scallions), cut into 4 cm (1½ inch) pieces, then finely shredded
lemon and garlic dipping sauce (page 36), to serve

SERVES 4–6

Wash the fish inside and out and pat dry with paper towel. Cut two diagonal slashes into the thickest part of the fish on both sides.

Put the peppercorns, chilli and fish sauce in a food processor and process until a paste is formed. Alternatively, use a mortar and pestle. Brush the paste lightly over the fish, cover and refrigerate for 20 minutes.

Heat the barbecue hotplate until very hot and lightly brush it with oil. Cook the fish for 8 minutes on each side, or until the flesh flakes easily when tested with a fork.

While the fish is cooking, heat the oil in a frying pan over medium heat. Add the onion and cook, stirring, for about 5 minutes, or until golden. Add the ginger, garlic and sugar and cook for a further 3 minutes.

Place the fish on a serving plate, top with the onion mixture, sprinkle over the spring onion and serve immediately with the lemon and garlic dipping sauce and steamed rice.

PREPARATION TIME: 20 MINUTES +   COOKING TIME: 25 MINUTES

CHILLI PORK KEBABS

500 g (1 lb 2 oz) pork fillet
2 tablespoons sweet chilli sauce
2 tablespoons tomato sauce (ketchup)
2 tablespoons hoisin sauce
2 garlic cloves, crushed
60 ml (2 fl oz/¼ cup) lemon juice
2 tablespoons honey
2 teaspoons grated fresh ginger
ready-made satay sauce, to serve

MAKES 8

Trim the fat and sinew from the pork, cut into small cubes and put into a non-metallic bowl.

Combine the sweet chilli sauce, tomato sauce, hoisin sauce, garlic, lemon juice, honey and ginger. Pour over the pork and stir well. Cover and refrigerate for several hours, or overnight.

Soak 8 wooden skewers in water for 30 minutes to ensure they don't burn during cooking. Thread the pork onto the skewers. Heat a little oil on a barbecue hotplate and cook the skewers for 3–4 minutes each side, or until cooked through. Brush with the remaining marinade while cooking. Serve with satay sauce.

PREPARATION TIME: 20 MINUTES +   COOKING TIME: 8 MINUTES

HONEYED PRAWN AND SCALLOP SKEWERS

500 g (1 lb 2 oz) raw prawns (shrimp)
250 g (9 oz) scallops

MARINADE
90 g (3¼ oz/¼ cup) honey
2 tablespoons soy sauce
60 ml (2 fl oz/¼ cup) barbecue sauce
2 tablespoons sweet sherry

MAKES 8

Soak 8 wooden skewers in water for 30 minutes to ensure they don't burn during cooking.

Meanwhile, peel the prawns, leaving the tails intact. Gently pull out the dark vein from each prawn back, starting at the head end. Slice or pull off any vein, membrane or hard white muscle from the scallops, leaving any roe attached. Thread the prawns and scallops alternately onto the skewers (about two prawns and three scallops per skewer). Place in a shallow non-metallic dish.

To make the marinade, combine the honey, soy sauce, barbecue sauce and sherry in a bowl and pour over the skewers. Cover and marinate in the refrigerator for 3 hours, or overnight.

Heat a little oil on a barbecue hotplate and cook the skewers, turning several times, for 5 minutes, or until cooked through. Brush frequently with the marinade while cooking.

PREPARATION TIME: 20 MINUTES +   COOKING TIME: 5 MINUTES

MARINATED OCTOPUS WITH SWEET CHILLI DRESSING

1 kg (2 lb 4 oz) baby octopus
125 ml (4 fl oz/½ cup) olive oil
2 garlic cloves, crushed
2 tablespoons finely chopped coriander (cilantro) leaves
1 red chilli, finely chopped
2 tablespoons lemon juice

SWEET CHILLI DRESSING
1 red chilli, finely chopped
60 ml (2 fl oz/¼ cup) lemon juice
2 tablespoons soft brown sugar
1 tablespoon fish sauce
2 tablespoons finely chopped coriander (cilantro) leaves
1 tablespoon sweet chilli sauce

SERVES 4–6

To clean the octopus, use a small sharp knife to cut off the head. Discard the head and gut. Pick up the octopus body and push up the beak with your index finger. Remove and discard the beak. Clean the octopus under running water and drain on crumpled paper towel.

In a non-metallic bowl, combine the oil, garlic, coriander, chilli and lemon juice. Add the octopus, mix well, then cover and refrigerate for at least 4 hours, or overnight.

To make the sweet chilli dressing, combine all the ingredients in a small jar and shake well.

Remove the octopus from the marinade and drain on crumpled paper towel. Heat the barbecue grill or hotplate to very hot and grease with oil. Cook the drained octopus, turning frequently, for 3–4 minutes, or until tender, basting with the marinade often to keep the octopus moist. Do not overcook, or the octopus will toughen. Serve either warm with the dressing, or cold as part of a salad.

PREPARATION TIME: 30 MINUTES +   COOKING TIME: 4 MINUTES

MALAYSIAN LAMB SKEWERS

500 g (1 lb 2 oz) lamb fillets
1 onion, roughly chopped
2 garlic cloves, crushed
2 cm (³/₄ inch) piece lemon grass, white part only, roughly chopped
2 slices fresh galangal
1 teaspoon chopped fresh ginger
1 teaspoon ground cumin
½ teaspoon ground fennel
1 tablespoon ground coriander
1 teaspoon ground turmeric
1 tablespoon soft brown sugar
1 tablespoon lemon juice

MAKES 8

Soak 8 wooden skewers in water for 30 minutes to ensure they don't burn during cooking.

Trim any fat or sinew from the lamb fillets. Slice the meat across the grain into very thin strips. (If you have time, leave the meat in the freezer for 30 minutes, as this will make it easier to thinly slice.)

In a food processor, combine the onion, garlic, lemon grass, galangal, ginger, cumin, fennel, coriander, turmeric, brown sugar and lemon juice and process until a smooth paste is formed. Transfer the paste to a shallow non-metallic dish and add the lamb, stirring to coat well. Cover and refrigerate overnight.

Thread the meat onto the skewers. Heat a little oil on a barbecue hotplate and cook the skewers for 3–4 minutes each side, or until cooked. Brush regularly with the remaining marinade while cooking.

PREPARATION TIME: 30 MINUTES +   COOKING TIME: 10 MINUTES

SPICY FISH KEBABS

1 kg (2 lb 4 oz) skinless firm fish fillets, such as swordfish or blue-eye
2 garlic cloves, crushed
160 g (5½ oz/²/₃ cup) Greek-style yoghurt
1 teaspoon chopped fresh ginger
1 red chilli, finely chopped
2 teaspoons garam masala
1 tablespoon chopped coriander (cilantro) leaves

SERVES 6

Soak 12 wooden skewers in water for 30 minutes to prevent them burning during cooking. Meanwhile, cut the fish into 3 cm (1¼ inch) cubes.

Combine the garlic, yoghurt, ginger, chilli, garam masala and coriander in a small bowl.

Thread the fish onto the skewers and place in a shallow dish. Spoon the marinade over the fish, cover and marinate in the refrigerator for 1 hour.

Heat a barbecue hotplate to hot and cook the skewers for 5–6 minutes, turning occasionally. Alternatively, cook the skewers under a hot grill (broiler). The fish is cooked when it flakes easily when tested with a fork. Serve with bread and a green salad.

PREPARATION TIME: 15 MINUTES +   COOKING TIME: 6 MINUTES

CHICKEN DRUMSTICKS WITH RANCH DRESSING

32 small chicken drumsticks
1 tablespoon garlic salt
1 tablespoon onion powder
oil, for deep-frying
250 ml (9 fl oz/1 cup) tomato sauce (ketchup)
80 ml (2½ fl oz/⅓ cup) worcestershire sauce
40 g (1½ oz) butter, melted
1 tablespoon sugar
Tabasco sauce, to taste

RANCH DRESSING
250 g (9 oz/1 cup) whole-egg mayonnaise
250 g (9 oz/1 cup) sour cream
80 ml (2½ fl oz/⅓ cup) lemon juice
20 g (¾ oz/⅓ cup) snipped chives

MAKES 32

Remove the skin from the chicken and use a cleaver or large knife to cut off the knuckle. Wash the chicken thoroughly and pat dry with paper towel. Combine 1 tablespoon freshly ground black pepper, the garlic salt and onion powder and rub some into each piece of chicken.

Fill a deep heavy-based frying pan or deep-fryer one-third full of oil and heat to 180°C (350°F), or until a cube of bread dropped into the oil turns golden brown in 15 seconds. Cook the chicken in batches for 2 minutes each batch, then remove with tongs or a slotted spoon and drain on paper towel.

Transfer the chicken to a large non-metallic bowl or shallow dish. Combine the tomato sauce, worcestershire sauce, butter, sugar and Tabasco sauce, pour over the chicken and stir to coat. Refrigerate the chicken, covered, for several hours, or overnight.

Heat the barbecue hotplate before cooking so it is very hot and grease with a little oil. Cook the chicken for 20–25 minutes, or until cooked through. Turn and brush with the marinade during cooking.

While the chicken is cooking, make the ranch dressing. Combine the mayonnaise, sour cream, lemon juice and chives and season to taste. Serve the chicken with the dressing.

PREPARATION TIME: 25 MINUTES +   COOKING TIME: 35 MINUTES

LEMON GRASS BEEF SKEWERS

500 g (1 lb 2 oz) sirloin steak
2 teaspoons chilli flakes
4 lemon grass stems, white part only,
chopped
2 slices fresh galangal, chopped
2 slices fresh turmeric, chopped
4 garlic cloves, peeled
1 tablespoon grated palm sugar (jaggery)
or soft brown sugar
125 ml (4 fl oz/1/2 cup) oyster sauce
2 tablespoons oil

SERVES 4

Soak 10–12 wooden skewers in water for 30 minutes to prevent them burning during cooking.

Cut the beef into long, thin strips and put in a non-metallic bowl. Using a mortar and pestle, pound the chilli, lemon grass, galangal, turmeric and garlic to form a paste. Add the sugar, oyster sauce, 1 teaspoon salt and the oil and combine well. Spoon the marinade over the beef and mix well. Cover with plastic wrap and refrigerate for 4 hours.

Thread the beef onto the skewers. Heat a barbecue grill or hotplate and cook the skewers for 5 minutes, or until browned and cooked through.

PREPARATION TIME: 15 MINUTES +   COOKING TIME: 5 MINUTES

CITRUS FISH WITH AVOCADO SALSA

4 firm fish cutlets, such as snapper,
salmon, jewfish or blue-eye
(about 185 g/6^1/2 oz each)
3 teaspoons finely grated orange zest
3 teaspoons finely grated lemon zest
1 tablespoon lime juice
2 tablespoons olive oil

AVOCADO SALSA
1^1/2 teaspoons ground cumin
1 small red chilli, seeded and
finely chopped
1 large avocado, finely chopped
1 red onion, very finely chopped
2 teaspoons lemon juice
2 teaspoons olive oil

SERVES 4

Put the fish in a shallow, non-metallic dish. Combine the orange zest, lemon zest, lime juice and olive oil in a small bowl and season with pepper. Pour over the fish and set aside to marinate for 5 minutes.

Heat and lightly oil a barbecue hotplate or grill and cook the fish for 3–5 minutes on each side, or until lightly browned and cooked through — the fish should flake easily when tested with a fork.

To make the avocado salsa, fry the cumin in a dry frying pan for about 40 seconds, shaking the pan constantly until fragrant. Combine the cumin with the chilli, avocado, onion, lemon juice and olive oil in a bowl. Serve the fish with the avocado salsa.

PREPARATION TIME: 30 MINUTES   COOKING TIME: 10 MINUTES

NOTE: Prepare the avocado salsa close to serving time so the avocado doesn't discolour.

MARINATED BARBECUED VEGETABLES

3 small slender eggplants (aubergines)
2 small red capsicums (peppers)
3 zucchini (courgettes)
6 mushrooms

MARINADE
60 ml (2 fl oz/¼ cup) olive oil
60 ml (2 fl oz/¼ cup) lemon juice
2 tablespoons shredded basil
1 garlic clove, crushed

SERVES 4–6

Cut the eggplants into diagonal slices. Place on a tray in a single layer, sprinkle with salt and set aside for 15 minutes. Rinse thoroughly and pat dry with paper towel. Halve the capsicums, remove the seeds and membrane and cut into long, wide pieces. Cut the zucchini into diagonal slices. Trim each mushroom stalk so that it is level with the cap. Place all the vegetables in a large, shallow non-metallic dish.

To make the marinade, combine the olive oil, lemon juice, basil and garlic in a bowl. Whisk until well combined. Pour the marinade over the vegetables and stir gently. Cover with plastic wrap and refrigerate for 1 hour, stirring occasionally.

Heat a barbecue grill and grease with a little oil. Place the vegetables on the hottest part of the barbecue and cook for 2 minutes on each side. Brush the vegetables frequently with any remaining marinade while cooking. Transfer to a serving dish once browned. Serve warm or at room temperature with barbecued meats.

PREPARATION TIME: 40 MINUTES +   COOKING TIME: 5 MINUTES

NOTES: Serve any leftovers with thick slices of crusty bread or bread rolls.

The vegetables can be marinated for up to 2 hours. Other herbs such as parsley, rosemary or thyme can be added to the marinade. Take the vegetables out of the refrigerator 15 minutes before cooking.

GARLIC PORK CHOPS

1 kg (2 lb 4 oz) pork chops
8 garlic cloves, crushed
2 tablespoons fish sauce
1 tablespoon soy sauce
2 tablespoons oyster sauce
2 tablespoons finely chopped
spring onion (scallion)

SERVES 4

Put the pork chops in a large glass bowl and add the garlic, fish sauce, soy sauce, oyster sauce and 1/2 teaspoon freshly ground black pepper. Stir well so that all the meat is covered with the marinade. Cover and marinate in the refrigerator for 4 hours.

Heat a barbecue grill or hotplate to hot and cook the pork on all sides until browned and cooked through. Alternatively you can cook the pork under a hot grill (broiler). If the pork starts to burn, move it further away from the grill element. Arrange the pork on a serving platter and scatter over the spring onion.

PREPARATION TIME: 10 MINUTES +   COOKING TIME: 15 MINUTES

BARBECUED QUAIL

6 quails
250 ml (9 fl oz/1 cup) dry red wine
2 celery stalks, including tops, chopped
1 carrot, chopped
1 small onion, chopped
1 bay leaf, torn into small pieces
1 teaspoon allspice
1 teaspoon dried thyme
2 garlic cloves, crushed
2 tablespoons olive oil
2 tablespoons lemon juice
lemon wedges, to serve

SERVES 4–6

To prepare the quails, use poultry shears to cut down either side of the backbone, then discard the backbone. Remove the innards and neck, wash the insides and pat dry with paper towel. Put the quails, breast side up, on the work surface, open out flat and gently press to flatten. Using poultry shears, cut in half through the breast, then cut each half in half again into the thigh and drumstick piece, and breast and wing piece. This will give you 24 pieces.

In a non-metallic bowl, combine the wine, celery, celery tops, carrot, onion, bay leaf and allspice. Add the quail and stir to coat. Cover and refrigerate for 3 hours, or preferably overnight, stirring occasionally. Drain and sprinkle with thyme, salt and pepper.

Whisk the garlic, olive oil and lemon juice in a small bowl. Heat a lightly oiled barbecue hotplate to very hot, then reduce the heat to medium. Cook the quail breast pieces for 4-5 minutes on each side and the drumstick pieces for 3 minutes each side, or until tender and cooked through. Brush frequently with the garlic and lemon mixture. Serve hot with lemon wedges.

PREPARATION TIME: 40 MINUTES +   COOKING TIME: 10 MINUTES

BARBECUED BEEF

500 g (1 lb 2 oz) scotch fillet or
sirloin steak
40 g (1¹/₂ oz/¹/₄ cup) sesame seeds
125 ml (4 fl oz/¹/₂ cup) soy sauce
2 garlic cloves, finely chopped
3 spring onions (scallions), finely chopped
1 tablespoon sesame oil
1 tablespoon vegetable oil
kimchi, to serve (see Note)

SERVES 4–6

Freeze the beef for 30 minutes. Remove from the freezer and slice into long, thin strips, cutting across the natural grain of the meat.

Toast the sesame seeds in a dry frying pan over medium heat for 3–4 minutes, shaking the pan gently, until the seeds are golden brown. Remove from the pan at once to prevent burning. Crush the seeds in a food mill or using a mortar and pestle.

Combine the beef, soy sauce, garlic, spring onion and half the sesame seeds in a bowl, mixing well. Cover and refrigerate for 2 hours.

Combine the sesame and vegetable oils and brush a little oil onto a chargrill pan, heavy-based frying pan or barbecue hotplate. Heat to very hot and cook the meat in three batches, searing each side for about 1 minute (don't overcook the beef or it will become chewy). Brush the pan with more oil and allow it to reheat to very hot between batches. Sprinkle the remaining crushed sesame seeds over the beef before serving. Serve with kimchi if desired.

PREPARATION TIME: 15 MINUTES +   COOKING TIME: 15 MINUTES

NOTE: Pickled vegetables are a popular accompaniment to meals in Korea. Most common is kimchi, made with pickled cabbage leaves and spiced with chilli. Ready-made kimchi is found in the refrigerator in Korean grocery stores and large Asian grocery stores.

PENNE SALAD WITH SUN-DRIED TOMATOES

500 g (1 lb 2 oz) penne pasta
1 tablespoon olive oil
150 g (5½ oz) sun-dried tomatoes, drained and thinly sliced
1 handful basil
80 g (2¾ oz/½ cup) pitted black olives, halved
2 tablespoons olive oil, extra
2 teaspoons white wine vinegar
1 garlic clove, halved
60 g (2¼ oz) parmesan cheese, shaved

SERVES 6

Cook the pasta in a large saucepan of boiling water until *al dente*. Drain and rinse under cold water, then drain again. Place in a large serving bowl and combine with the oil to prevent sticking. Mix the tomatoes, basil and olives into the pasta.

Combine the extra olive oil, vinegar and garlic in a small jar and shake well. Leave for 5 minutes, then discard the garlic. Shake the dressing again and pour over the salad. Stir gently to combine. Garnish with parmesan and serve immediately.

PREPARATION TIME: 15 MINUTES   COOKING TIME: 10 MINUTES

ROCKET, TOMATO AND SALAMI PASTA SALAD

350 g (12 oz) orecchiette pasta
6 slices spicy Italian salami, cut into strips
150 g (5½ oz) rocket (arugula), shredded
200 g (7 oz) cherry tomatoes, halved
80 ml (2½ fl oz/⅓ cup) olive oil
60 ml (2 fl oz/¼ cup) white wine vinegar
1 teaspoon sugar

SERVES 6

Cook the pasta in a large saucepan of boiling water until *al dente*. Drain and rinse under cold water, then drain again. Allow to cool.

Heat a frying pan over medium heat, add the salami and cook until crisp. Drain well on paper towel. Combine the salami, pasta, rocket and cherry tomatoes in a large bowl.

In a small food processor, combine the olive oil, vinegar, sugar and ¼ teaspoon each of salt and pepper. Process for 1 minute. Drizzle the dressing over the salad just before serving.

PREPARATION TIME: 15 MINUTES   COOKING TIME: 15 MINUTES

Penne salad with sun-dried tomatoes

CITRUS WALNUT SALAD

2 oranges
2 grapefruit
125 g (4$^1/_2$ oz) sugar snap peas
75 g (2$^1/_2$ oz) rocket (arugula), leaves torn
$^1/_2$ oak leaf lettuce, leaves torn
1 large Lebanese (short) cucumber, sliced
40 g (1$^1/_2$ oz/$^1/_3$ cup) walnut pieces

WALNUT DRESSING
2 tablespoons walnut oil
2 tablespoons oil
2 teaspoons tarragon vinegar
2 teaspoons seeded mustard
1 teaspoon sweet chilli sauce

SERVES 8

Peel the oranges and grapefruit, removing all the white pith. Cut the fruit into segments between the membranes, removing the seeds.

Cover the sugar snap peas with boiling water and set aside for 2 minutes. Drain and then plunge the snap peas into iced water. Drain and pat dry with paper towel.

Combine the oranges, grapefruit, snap peas, rocket, lettuce, cucumber and walnut pieces in a large bowl.

To make the walnut dressing, combine all the ingredients in a jar and shake well. Pour the dressing over the salad and toss until combined.

PREPARATION TIME: 20 MINUTES   COOKING TIME: NIL

BABY ZUCCHINI SALAD

1 kg (2 lb 4 oz) small zucchini (courgettes),
ends trimmed
1 small red onion, thinly sliced
3 tablespoons chopped flat-leaf
(Italian) parsley

OIL AND LEMON DRESSING
125 ml (4 fl oz/^{1}/$_2$ cup) olive oil
60 ml (2 fl oz/^{1}/$_4$ cup) lemon
2 teaspoons chopped oregano

SERVES 6–8

Cook the whole zucchini in boiling salted water for 5 minutes, or until just tender. Drain and place in a bowl with the onion and parsley.

To make the oil and lemon dressing, combine the olive oil, lemon juice and oregano in a jar. Season with salt and pepper and shake to combine. Drizzle the dressing over the zucchini and toss to combine. Serve at room temperature with barbecued meats or fish.

PREPARATION TIME: 10 MINUTES   COOKING TIME: 5 MINUTES

CAPSICUM SALAD

1 large red capsicum (pepper)
1 large green capsicum (pepper)
1 large yellow capsicum (pepper)
1 tablespoon olive oil
2 tablespoons green peppercorns
155 g (5^1/$_2$ oz/1 cup) kalamata olives
2 tablespoons mint
1 tablespoon raspberry vinegar
rocket (arugula) leaves, to serve

SERVES 4–6

Cut the capsicums into quarters, then remove the seeds and membrane. Put the capsicum quarters, skin side up, under a hot grill (broiler). Cook until the skin blackens and blisters. Remove from the grill and put in a plastic bag until cool, then peel off the skin.

Cut the capsicums into thick strips and put in a bowl with the olive oil, peppercorns and olives. Stir through the mint and raspberry vinegar. Serve on a bed of rocket leaves.

PREPARATION TIME: 15 MINUTES   COOKING TIME: 10 MINUTES

Baby zucchini salad

WILD AND BROWN RICE SALAD

95 g (3¼ oz/½ cup) wild rice
200 g (7 oz/1 cup) brown rice
1 red onion, finely chopped
1 small red capsicum (pepper),
finely chopped
2 celery stalks, thinly sliced
2 tablespoons chopped flat-leaf
(Italian) parsley
4 tablespoons chopped pecans

CITRUS DRESSING
60 ml (2 fl oz/¼ cup) orange juice
60 ml (2 fl oz/¼ cup) lemon juice
1 teaspoon finely grated orange zest
1 teaspoon finely grated lemon zest
80 ml (2½ fl oz/⅓ cup) olive oil

SERVES 6

Cook the wild rice in a saucepan of boiling water for 30–40 minutes until just tender. Drain well and allow to cool completely. Meanwhile, boil the brown rice for 25–30 minutes, drain well and allow to cool.

Combine the onion, capsicum, celery and parsley in a bowl with the cooked rice.

Place the pecans in a dry frying pan and stir over medium heat for 2–3 minutes until lightly toasted. Transfer to a plate to cool.

To make the dressing, put the orange juice, lemon juice, zest and olive oil in a small jar and shake well to combine. Pour the dressing over the rice salad and gently fold through. Add the pecans and gently combine. Serve with pitta or crusty bread if desired.

PREPARATION TIME: 20 MINUTES   COOKING TIME: 40 MINUTES

WARM BEAN SALAD

2 tablespoons olive oil
1 onion, finely chopped
1 garlic clove, crushed
1 small red capsicum (pepper), cut into short strips
90 g (3¼ oz) green beans
60 g (2¼ oz) button mushrooms, sliced
1 tablespoon balsamic vinegar
440 g (15½ oz) tinned mixed beans, drained and rinsed
chopped flat-leaf (Italian) parsley, to serve

SERVES 4

Heat half the olive oil in a frying pan over medium heat. Add the onion and cook for 2 minutes, then add the garlic, capsicum, beans, mushrooms and vinegar. Cook for another 5 minutes, stirring occasionally.

Add the mixed beans to the vegetables along with the remaining oil and stir until just warmed through. Sprinkle with the parsley.

PREPARATION TIME: 10 MINUTES   COOKING TIME: 8 MINUTES

NACHOS SALAD

440 g (15½ oz) tinned red kidney beans, drained and rinsed
1 large tomato, cubed
125 g (4½ oz/½ cup) mild salsa
280 g (10 oz) packet plain corn chips
8 lettuce leaves, shredded
1 small avocado, sliced
20 g (¾ oz) cheddar cheese, grated

SERVES 4

Combine the kidney beans, tomato and salsa in a bowl.

Arrange a bed of corn chips on each plate and top with lettuce, the bean mixture and avocado. Sprinkle with the grated cheese and serve.

PREPARATION TIME: 15 MINUTES   COOKING TIME: NIL

SIMPLY JAPANESE

SUSHI HAND-ROLLS

220 g (7³/4 oz/1 cup) Japanese
short-grain rice
1 tablespoon rice vinegar
2 teaspoons caster (superfine) sugar
175 g (6 oz) sashimi-grade fish, such
as tuna or salmon
6 sheets roasted nori (dried seaweed),
20 x 18 cm (8 x 7 inches) (see Note)
1 small avocado
1 tablespoon lemon juice
wasabi paste
60 g (2¹/4 oz) pickled daikon
85 g (3 oz) cucumber, cut into thin strips
Japanese soy sauce, to serve
pickled ginger, to serve

MAKES 12

Wash the rice under cold running water until the water runs clear, then
drain thoroughly. Leave the rice in the strainer to drain for 1 hour. Put
the rice in a saucepan and cover with 300 ml (10¹/2 fl oz) water. Cover the
pan and bring the water to the boil, then reduce the heat to very low and
simmer for 10 minutes. Remove the pan from the heat, remove the lid and
put a clean cloth across the top to absorb excess moisture. Set aside for
10 minutes.

To make the sushi dressing, combine the vinegar, sugar and ¹/4 teaspoon
salt in a small bowl.

Spread the rice over the base of a non-metallic dish or bowl, pour the
sushi dressing over the top and use a rice paddle or spatula to mix the
dressing through the rice. Fan the rice until it cools to room temperature.
Cover with a damp cloth and set it aside, but do not refrigerate.

Meanwhile, using a sharp knife, cut the fish into 12 paper-thin pieces,
measuring 2 x 5 cm (³/4 x 2 inches). Using scissors, cut each sheet of nori
in half. Thinly slice the avocado and sprinkle with a little lemon juice.

Use wet hands to stop the rice sticking to your fingers as you form the
sushi. Taking 1 heaped tablespoon of rice at a time, mould the rice into
oval shapes — you should end up with 12 ovals.

Smear a little wasabi on a piece of nori. Then, holding the nori in the
palm of your hand, put an oval of rice on top, then a piece of fish,
avocado, daikon and cucumber. Wrap the nori around the ingredients in
a cone shape, using a couple of grains of cooked rice to secure the rolls.
Repeat with the remaining pieces of nori and fillings. Alternatively, put
the ingredients on the table for guests to help themselves. Serve with
the soy sauce for dipping, extra wasabi and pickled ginger.

PREPARATION TIME: 25 MINUTES +   COOKING TIME: 15 MINUTES

NOTE: Nori is the most common form of dried seaweed used
in Japanese cookery. Nori sheets are available from Asian grocery
stores and large supermarkets.

CHICKEN WITH NORI

400 g (14 oz) chicken breast tenderloins
60 ml (2 fl oz/^{1}/$_4$ cup) Japanese
soy sauce
60 ml (2 fl oz/^{1}/$_4$ cup) mirin
4 cm (1^1/$_2$ inch) piece fresh ginger, very
finely grated
1 sheet nori (dried seaweed), finely
chopped or crumbled into
very small pieces
40 g (1^1/$_2$ oz/^{1}/$_3$ cup) cornflour
(cornstarch)
250 ml (9 fl oz/1 cup) oil, for frying

MAKES ABOUT 30 PIECES

Carefully trim and discard any sinew from the chicken, then cut the chicken into bite-sized pieces and put them in a bowl.

Combine the soy sauce, mirin and ginger in a small bowl, then pour over the chicken and toss to coat the chicken. Marinate in the refrigerator for 15 minutes, then drain off any excess marinade. Mix the nori with the cornflour and, using your fingertips, lightly coat the chicken in the cornflour and nori.

Put the oil in a deep heavy-based saucepan or deep-fryer and heat to 180°C (350°F), or until a cube of bread dropped into the oil turns golden brown in 15 seconds. Fry six or seven pieces of chicken at a time until golden, turning regularly. Drain on crumpled paper towel. Garnish with extra strips of nori if desired.

PREPARATION TIME: 25 MINUTES   COOKING TIME: 20 MINUTES

SMOKED SALMON RICE BALLS

275 g (9^3/$_4$ oz/1^1/$_4$ cups) Japanese
short-grain rice
55 g (2 oz) smoked salmon, chopped
2 tablespoons finely chopped
pickled ginger
2 spring onions (scallions), finely chopped
2 teaspoons black sesame seeds, toasted

MAKES ABOUT 20 BALLS

Wash the rice under cold running water until the water runs clear, then drain thoroughly. Leave the rice in the strainer to drain for 1 hour. Put the rice in a saucepan with 330 ml (11^1/$_4$ fl oz/1^1/$_3$ cups) water. Cover the pan and bring to the boil, then reduce the heat to very low and simmer for 10 minutes. Remove the pan from the heat, remove the lid and put a clean cloth across the top to absorb excess moisture. Set aside for 10 minutes.

Combine the salmon, ginger and spring onion in a small bowl. Using wet hands, form 1 heaped tablespoon of rice into a ball, push 2 teaspoons of the salmon mixture into the centre of the rice and remould the ball around it. Repeat with the remaining rice and salmon, keeping your hands wet to prevent the rice from sticking. Sprinkle with the sesame seeds.

PREPARATION TIME: 20 MINUTES +   COOKING TIME: 15 MINUTES

CALIFORNIA ROLLS

220 g (7³/4 oz/1 cup) Japanese
short-grain rice
1 tablespoon rice vinegar
2 teaspoons caster (superfine) sugar
1 large egg
1 teaspoon sake
a pinch of caster (superfine) sugar
1 teaspoon oil
2 sheets roasted nori (dried seaweed),
20 x 18 cm (8 x 7 inches)
2 crabsticks, 40 g (1¹/2 oz) each,
cut into strips
25 g (1 oz) pickled daikon, cut into
matchsticks
25 g (1 oz) carrot, cut into
matchsticks
25 g (1 oz) cucumber, cut into
matchsticks
Japanese soy sauce, to serve
wasabi paste, to serve
pickled ginger, to serve

MAKES 12

Wash the rice under cold running water until the water runs clear, then drain thoroughly. Leave the rice in the strainer to drain for 1 hour. Put the rice in a saucepan and cover with 300 ml (7¹/2 fl oz) water. Cover the pan and bring the water to the boil, then reduce the heat to very low and simmer for 10 minutes. Remove the pan from the heat, remove the lid and put a clean cloth across the top to absorb excess moisture. Set aside for 10 minutes.

To make the sushi dressing, combine the vinegar, sugar and ¹/4 teaspoon salt in a small bowl.

Spread the rice over the base of a non-metallic dish or bowl, pour the sushi dressing over the top and use a rice paddle or spatula to mix the dressing through the rice, separating the grains as you do so. Fan the rice until it cools to room temperature. Cover with a damp cloth and set it aside, but do not refrigerate.

To make the omelette, gently combine the egg, sake, the pinch of sugar and a pinch of salt. Heat the oil in a small frying pan over medium heat. Add the egg mixture and cook until firm around the edges but still slightly soft in the middle. Roll up the omelette, then tip it out of the pan. Cool, then slice into strips.

Put a nori sheet on a sushi mat, with the nori shiny side down. Top with half the rice, spreading it over the nori, leaving a 2 cm (³/4 inch) gap at the edge furthest away from you. Lay half of the fillings on the rice in the following order: omelette, crabstick, daikon, carrot and cucumber. Starting with the end nearest to you, tightly roll up the mat and the nori, making sure you do not tuck the edge of the mat under the roll. Repeat this process with the remaining ingredients.

Using a sharp knife, trim the ends and cut each roll into six slices. After cutting each slice, rinse the knife under cold water to prevent sticking. Serve with soy sauce, wasabi and pickled ginger.

PREPARATION TIME: 25 MINUTES +   COOKING TIME: 20 MINUTES

CHICKEN TERIYAKI

80 ml (2¹/₂ fl oz/¹/₃ cup) mirin
80 ml (2¹/₂ fl oz/¹/₃ cup) Japanese soy sauce
60 g (2¹/₄ oz/¹/₃ cup) soft brown sugar
1 tablespoon finely chopped fresh ginger
2 small garlic cloves, crushed
500 g (1 lb 2 oz) boneless, skinless chicken breasts, cut into 3 cm (1¹/₄ inch) cubes
60 ml (2 fl oz/¹/₄ cup) peanut oil
10 spring onions (scallions), cut into 3 cm (1¹/₄ inch) lengths

SERVES 4

Combine the mirin, soy sauce, sugar, ginger and garlic in a large shallow non-metallic dish and stir to dissolve the sugar. Add the chicken and toss well. Marinate for 10 minutes.

Drain the chicken, reserving the marinade. Add the peanut oil to the marinade. Thread the chicken onto 12 metal skewers, alternating with the spring onions. Brush with the marinade.

Put the chicken on an oiled tray and cook under a hot grill (broiler) for 2 minutes. Turn over and brush with more marinade. Cook for 5 minutes, or until the chicken is cooked through.

Put any remaining marinade in a small saucepan over medium heat and bring to the boil. Serve the chicken with rice, and the marinade on the side.

PREPARATION TIME: 20 MINUTES + COOKING TIME: 10 MINUTES

SASHIMI SALMON AND CUCUMBER ROLLS

200 g (7 oz) sashimi-grade salmon fillet
1 small Lebanese (short) cucumber
25 trimmed chives
Japanese soy sauce, to serve
pickled ginger, to serve
wasabi paste, to serve

MAKES 25

Cut the salmon into paper-thin slices, on an angle. Cut the cucumber in half and scoop out the seeds with a teaspoon, then cut the flesh into long, thin strips.

Place a salmon slice on a board, top with strips of cucumber, then roll up and tie with the chives. Serve with soy sauce for dipping, and pickled ginger and wasabi.

NOTE: Japanese soy sauce, or shoyu, is a much lighter and sweeter sauce than the Chinese one. It should be refrigerated after opening.

Chicken teriyaki

TUNA SUSHI ROLLS

220 g (7³/₄ oz/1 cup) Japanese
short-grain rice
1 tablespoon rice vinegar
2 teaspoons caster (superfine) sugar
150 g (5¹/₂ oz) sashimi-grade tuna
¹/₂ Lebanese (short) cucumber
¹/₂ avocado
4 sheets roasted nori (dried seaweed),
20 x 18 cm (8 x 7 inches)
wasabi paste
pickled ginger, to serve
Japanese soy sauce, to serve

MAKES 24

Wash the rice under cold running water until the water runs clear, then drain thoroughly. Leave the rice in the strainer to drain for 1 hour. Put the rice in a saucepan and cover with 300 ml (10¹/₂ fl oz) water. Cover the pan and bring the water to the boil, then reduce the heat to very low and simmer for 10 minutes. Remove the pan from the heat, remove the lid and put a clean cloth across the top to absorb excess moisture. Set aside for 10 minutes.

To make the sushi dressing, combine the vinegar, sugar and ¹/₄ teaspoon salt in a small bowl.

Spread the rice over the base of a non-metallic dish or bowl, pour the sushi dressing over the top and use a rice paddle or spatula to mix the dressing through the rice, separating the grains as you do so. Fan the rice until it cools to room temperature. Cover with a damp cloth and set it aside, but do not refrigerate.

Cut the tuna, cucumber and avocado into thin strips. Put a nori sheet on a sushi mat, with the nori shiny side down. Spread a quarter of the rice over the nori, leaving a 2 cm (³/₄ inch) gap at the edge furthest away from you. Spread a small amount of wasabi along the centre of the rice, then add the strips of tuna, cucumber and avocado. Starting with the end nearest to you, tightly roll up the mat and the nori, making sure you do not tuck the edge of the mat under the roll. Push in any rice that is escaping from the ends. Repeat with the remaining ingredients.

Wet a sharp knife, trim the ends of each roll and cut the roll in half and then each half into three. Serve with ginger, and soy sauce for dipping.

PREPARATION TIME: 25 MINUTES + COOKING TIME: 15 MINUTES

HAND-SHAPED TUNA SUSHI

220 g (7³/4 oz/1 cup) Japanese
short-grain rice
1 tablespoon rice vinegar
2 teaspoons caster (superfine) sugar
300 g (10¹/2 oz) sashimi-grade tuna
wasabi paste
Japanese soy sauce, to serve

MAKES ABOUT 20

Wash the rice under cold running water until the water runs clear, then drain thoroughly. Leave the rice in the strainer to drain for 1 hour. Put the rice in a saucepan and cover with 300 ml (10¹/2 fl oz) water. Cover the pan and bring the water to the boil, then reduce the heat to very low and simmer for 10 minutes. Remove the pan from the heat, remove the lid and put a clean cloth across the top to absorb excess moisture. Set aside for 10 minutes.

To make the sushi dressing, combine the vinegar, sugar and ¹/4 teaspoon salt in a small bowl.

Spread the rice over the base of a non-metallic dish or bowl, pour the sushi dressing over the top and use a rice paddle or spatula to mix the dressing through the rice. Fan the rice until it cools to room temperature. Cover with a damp cloth and set it aside, but do not refrigerate.

Cut the tuna into thin strips about 5 cm (2 inches) long, then put a dab of wasabi on each.

With wet hands, roll 1 tablespoon of rice into a ball. Place the rice ball onto a strip of tuna, with the wasabi side against the rice, and then gently mould the tuna around the rice. Flatten the ball slightly to elongate it, then lay the balls on a tray, seam side down. Repeat with the rest of the ingredients. Serve with soy sauce and wasabi. If desired, stir a little of the wasabi into the soy sauce.

PREPARATION TIME: 20 MINUTES +   COOKING TIME: 15 MINUTES

SUSHI CREPES

4 eggs
220 g (7³/₄ oz/1 cup) Japanese
short-grain rice
1 tablespoon rice vinegar
2 teaspoons caster (superfine) sugar
wasabi paste
125 g (4¹/₂ oz) sashimi-grade tuna,
cut into thin strips
1 small Lebanese (short) cucumber,
peeled and cut into matchsticks
¹/₂ avocado, cut into matchsticks
3 tablespoons pickled ginger,
cut into thin strips
Japanese soy sauce, to serve

MAKES ABOUT 40

To make the egg crepes, gently whisk the eggs with 2 tablespoons cold water and a pinch of salt in a bowl until combined. Lightly oil a small crepe pan and heat over low heat. Pour enough of the egg mixture into the pan to lightly cover the base and cook for 1 minute, being careful not to allow the crepe to brown. Turn the crepe over and cook for 1 minute. Transfer to a plate and cook the remaining mixture.

Wash the rice under cold running water until the water runs clear, then drain thoroughly. Leave the rice in the strainer to drain for 1 hour. Put the rice in a saucepan and cover with 300 ml (10¹/₂ fl oz) water. Cover the pan and bring the water to the boil, then reduce the heat to very low and simmer for 10 minutes. Remove the pan from the heat, remove the lid and put a clean cloth across the top to absorb excess moisture. Set aside for 10 minutes.

To make the sushi dressing, combine the vinegar, sugar and ¹/₄ teaspoon salt in a small bowl.

Spread the rice over the base of a non-metallic dish or bowl, pour the sushi dressing over the top and use a rice paddle or spatula to mix the dressing through the rice. Fan the rice until it cools to room temperature.

Place one egg crepe on a sushi mat or a piece of baking paper. Spread 4 tablespoons of the sushi rice over a third of the crepe, using a spatula or the back of a spoon. Spread a tiny amount of wasabi along the centre of the rice. Put some tuna, cucumber, avocado and ginger over the wasabi. Using the sushi mat or paper to help you, fold the crepe over to enclose the filling and roll up firmly in the mat or paper. Repeat with the remaining crepes and filling ingredients. Trim the ends with a knife and then cut the crepe rolls into 2 cm (³/₄ inch) rounds. Serve with soy sauce.

PREPARATION TIME: 1 HOUR   COOKING TIME: 30 MINUTES

NOTE: Sashimi tuna is the freshest, highest quality tuna and is available from good seafood outlets.

MIXED SASHIMI

500 g (1 lb 2 oz) sashimi-grade fish, such as tuna, salmon, kingfish, ocean trout, snapper, whiting, bream or jewfish
1 carrot, peeled
1 daikon, peeled
Japanese soy sauce, to serve
wasabi paste, to serve

Use a very sharp, flat-bladed knife to remove any skin from the fish. Place the fish in the freezer and chill it until it is just firm enough to be cut thinly and evenly into slices, about 5 mm (1/4 inch) in width. Try to make each cut one motion in one direction, taking care not to saw the fish.

Use a zester to scrape the carrot and daikon into long fine strips, or cut them into thin matchstick strips. Arrange the sashimi on a platter. Garnish with the carrot and daikon and serve with the soy sauce and wasabi.

SERVES 4   PREPARATION TIME: 30 MINUTES   COOKING TIME: NIL

INARI SUSHI

220 g (7³/4 oz/1 cup) Japanese short-grain rice
1 tablespoon rice vinegar
2 teaspoons caster (superfine) sugar
1 teaspoon mirin
8 inari pouches (see Note)
2 tablespoons white sesame seeds, toasted
pickled ginger, to serve

MAKES 8

Wash the rice under cold running water until the water runs clear, then drain thoroughly. Leave the rice in the strainer to drain for 1 hour. Put the rice in a saucepan and cover with 300 ml (10¹/2 fl oz) water. Cover the pan and bring the water to the boil, then reduce the heat to very low and simmer for 10 minutes. Remove the pan from the heat, remove the lid and put a clean cloth across the top to absorb excess moisture. Set aside for 10 minutes.

To make the sushi dressing, combine the rice vinegar, sugar, mirin and 1/4 teaspoon salt in a small bowl.

Spread the rice over the base of a non-metallic dish or bowl, pour the sushi dressing over the top and use a rice paddle or spatula to mix the dressing through the rice. Fan the rice until it cools to room temperature.

Gently separate the inari pockets and open them up. Form the rice into balls and place inside each pocket. Sprinkle the rice with the toasted sesame seeds and press the inari closed. Serve on a plate, cut side down, with pickled ginger.

REPARATION TIME: 20 MINUTES +   COOKING TIME: 15 MINUTES

NOTE: Inari pouches (*aburage*) are slightly sweet pockets made from deep-fried tofu. They are available from Japanese grocery stores.

STEAMED SAKE CHICKEN

500 g (1 lb 2 oz) boneless chicken breasts,
with skin on
80 ml (2¹/₂ fl oz/¹/₃ cup) sake
2 tablespoons lemon juice
4 cm (1¹/₂ inch) piece fresh ginger,
cut into very thin matchsticks

SAUCE
2 tablespoons Japanese soy sauce
1 tablespoon mirin
1 teaspoon sesame oil
1 spring onion (scallion), sliced

GARNISH
2 spring onions (scallions)
¹/₂ small red capsicum (pepper)

SERVES 4

Use a fork to prick the skin on the chicken in several places. Put the chicken, skin side up, in a shallow dish and sprinkle with 1 teaspoon salt. Combine the sake, lemon juice and ginger in a bowl. Pour over the chicken, then cover and marinate in the refrigerator for 30–40 minutes.

To make the sauce, combine the soy sauce, mirin, sesame oil and spring onion in a small bowl.

To make the garnish, peel the outside layer from the spring onions, then cut finely into diagonal pieces. Lay the capsicum flat on a board, skin side down. Holding a knife in a horizontal position, cut just under the membrane surface to remove the top layer, then discard it. Cut the capsicum into very thin 3 cm (1¹/₄ inch) long strips.

Line the base of a bamboo or metal steamer with baking paper. Remove the chicken from the marinade and arrange it, skin side up, in the steamer. Fill a wok or frying pan with 500 ml (17 fl oz/2 cups) water and bring to the boil. Sit the steamer in the wok, cover and cook over gently boiling water for 15–20 minutes, or until the chicken is cooked.

Cut the chicken into bite-sized pieces (remove the skin if you prefer) and arrange in the centre of a serving plate. Drizzle over the sauce. Arrange the capsicum strips in a bundle on the side of the plate and scatter the spring onion over the chicken. Serve warm or cold, with rice if desired.

PREPARATION TIME: 25 MINUTES +   COOKING TIME: 20 MINUTES

JAPANESE CRUMBED PRAWNS

18 raw large prawns (shrimp)
2 tablespoons cornflour (cornstarch)
3 eggs
120 g (4¼ oz/2 cups) Japanese breadcrumbs (panko)
peanut oil, for deep-frying
80 ml (2½ fl oz/⅓ cup) ponzu sauce (see Note)

MAKES 18

Peel the prawns, leaving the tails intact. Cut down the back of each prawn to form a butterfly, then place between two layers of plastic wrap and beat gently to form a cutlet.

Put the cornflour, eggs and breadcrumbs in separate bowls. Lightly beat the eggs. Dip each prawn first into the cornflour, then into the egg and finally into the breadcrumbs, ensuring that each cutlet is well covered in crumbs.

Fill a wok one-third full of oil and heat to 180°C (350°F), or until a cube of bread dropped into the oil turns golden brown in 15 seconds. Cook six prawn cutlets at a time for about 1 minute each side, or until the crumbs are golden — be careful they don't burn. Serve with ponzu sauce.

PREPARATION TIME: 15 MINUTES   COOKING TIME: 10 MINUTES

NOTE: If ponzu isn't available, mix 60 ml (2 fl oz/¼ cup) soy sauce with 1 tablespoon lemon juice.

CRAB AND PRAWN NORI ROLLS

170 g (6 oz) tinned crabmeat
350 g (12 oz) peeled and deveined raw prawns (shrimp)
1 egg white
2 teaspoons finely grated fresh ginger
2 tablespoons chopped coriander (cilantro) leaves
1 spring onion (scallion), finely chopped
2 sheets nori (dried seaweed), toasted
coriander (cilantro) leaves, to garnish

MAKES 16

Drain the crabmeat and put into a food processor with the prawns, egg white and ginger and process until smooth. Add the coriander and spring onion and process until just combined. Season with salt and pepper.

Divide the mixture between the nori sheets and spread evenly over the sheets. Roll up to enclose the filling. Using a sharp knife, cut each roll into eight rounds, wiping the knife clean between slices.

Place the rolls 2 cm (¾ inch) apart in a lightly oiled bamboo or metal steamer. Steam over a large wok or saucepan of simmering water for about 5 minutes, or until just cooked. Garnish the rolls with a coriander leaf and serve warm.

PREPARATION TIME: 15 MINUTES   COOKING TIME: 5 MINUTES

STUFFED SHIITAKE

STUFFING
300 g (10½ oz) raw prawns (shrimp)
150 g (5½ oz) minced (ground) chicken
50 g (1¾ oz) pork fat (ask your butcher), very finely chopped
30 g (1 oz) ham, finely chopped
1 spring onion (scallion), finely chopped
2 large garlic cloves, crushed
1½ tablespoons finely chopped water chestnuts
1½ tablespoons finely chopped bamboo shoots
1½ teaspoons grated fresh ginger
1 tablespoon Chinese rice wine
1 tablespoon oyster sauce
1 tablespoon light soy sauce
2-3 drops sesame oil
1 egg white, beaten until frothy
¼ teaspoon sugar
pinch Chinese five-spice
white pepper

300 g (10½ oz) fresh shiitake mushrooms (see Note)
1 litre (35 fl oz/4 cups) chicken stock
1 star anise
oyster sauce, to serve
sesame seeds, toasted, to garnish

SERVES 4–6

To make the stuffing, peel the prawns. Gently pull out the dark vein from each prawn back, starting at the head end. Finely chop the prawn meat and put it in a bowl with the chicken, pork fat, ham, spring onion, garlic, water chestnuts, bamboo shoots, ginger, rice wine, oyster sauce, soy sauce, sesame oil, egg white, sugar, five-spice and white pepper and mix together thoroughly.

Remove the stalks from the shiitake and reserve. Generously fill each mushroom cap with the stuffing, rounding the tops slightly. The amount of stuffing you use for each mushroom will differ depending on their size — if the mushrooms are very small you may have some mixture left over.

Pour the stock and 500 ml (17 fl oz/2 cups) water into a wok and add the star anise and reserved mushroom stalks. Bring to the boil over high heat, then reduce to a simmer. Line a large bamboo steamer with baking paper and put the mushrooms, filling side up, in a single layer on top. Sit the steamer in the wok. Cover and steam over gently boiling water for about 15 minutes, or until the filling and the mushrooms are cooked through.

Place on a serving platter and pour over a little of the broth. Drizzle with a little oyster sauce and sprinkle with toasted sesame seeds.

PREPARATION TIME: 30 MINUTES   COOKING TIME: 20 MINUTES

NOTE: When buying fresh shiitake, choose mushrooms that are plump, with firm caps that curl under. Ignore any with shrivelled, dehydrated caps as they are well past their peak. Choose ones of similar size so they cook evenly.

MIXED TEMPURA

12 raw king prawns (shrimp)
1 sheet nori (dried seaweed), cut into
12 thin strips
250 g (9 oz/2 cups) tempura flour
(see Notes)
500 ml (17 fl oz/2 cups) iced water
2 egg yolks, lightly beaten
oil, for deep-frying
flour, for coating
60 g (2¼ oz) broccoli florets
100 g (3½ oz) button mushrooms
1 red capsicum (pepper), cut into
2 cm (¾ inch) strips
Japanese soy sauce, to serve

MAKES ABOUT 30

Peel the prawns, leaving the tails intact. Gently pull out the dark vein from each prawn back, starting at the head end. Cut a slit in the underside of each prawn (this will prevent them curling) and wrap a piece of nori around the base of the tail.

Sift the flour into a bowl, make a well in the centre and add the iced water and egg yolk. Stir with chopsticks until just combined. The batter should be slightly lumpy.

Fill a deep heavy-based saucepan one-third full of oil and heat to 180°C (350°F), or until a cube of bread dropped into the oil turns golden brown in 15 seconds.

Dip the prawns in flour to coat, shake off any excess, then dip in the batter. Drain off the excess, then lower the prawns into the oil and deep-fry in batches until crisp and light golden. Drain on crumpled paper towel. Repeat with the vegetables. Serve the tempura immediately with soy sauce for dipping.

PREPARATION TIME: 20 MINUTES   COOKING TIME: 15 MINUTES

NOTES: Tempura should have a very light batter and needs to be served as soon as it is cooked. Be sure that the water is ice cold as this helps to lighten the batter. If you are unsure, add a few ice cubes.

Buy tempura flour at Asian supermarkets. If unavailable, use 90 g (3¼ oz/½ cup) rice flour and 185 g (6½ oz/1½ cups) plain (all-purpose) flour.

PRAWN, NOODLE AND NORI PARCELS

1 kg (2 lb 4 oz) raw prawns (shrimp)
250 g (9 oz) dried somen noodles
2 sheets nori (dried seaweed)
60 g (2¼ oz/½ cup) plain (all-purpose) flour
2 egg yolks
oil, for deep-frying

DIPPING SAUCE
80 ml (2½ fl oz/⅓ cup) tonkatsu sauce or barbecue sauce
2 tablespoons lemon juice
1 tablespoon sake or mirin
1–2 teaspoons grated fresh ginger

MAKES ABOUT 24

Peel the prawns, leaving the tails intact. Gently pull out the dark vein from each prawn back, starting at the head end. Set aside.

Using a sharp knife, cut the noodles to the same length as the prawn bodies, to the base of the tail. Keep the noodles in neat bundles and set aside. Cut the nori into 2.5 cm (1 inch) wide strips.

Sift the flour into a large bowl and make a well in the centre. Mix the egg yolks with 3 tablespoons water. Gradually add to the flour, whisking to make a smooth, lump-free batter. Add another tablespoon of water if the mixture is too thick. Set aside.

To make the dipping sauce, combine the ingredients in a small bowl, adding the ginger according to taste.

Dip a prawn in the batter, letting the excess run off, then roll the prawn lengthways in the noodles to coat it with a single layer of noodles. Secure the noodles by rolling a nori strip around the centre of the prawn and securing the seaweed with a little batter. Repeat with the remaining prawns, noodles and nori strips.

Fill a deep heavy-based saucepan or wok one-third full of oil and heat to 180°C (350°F), or until a cube of bread dropped into the oil turns golden brown in 15 seconds. Deep-fry two or three coated prawns at a time, for 1–2 minutes, or until the prawns are cooked. Drain on crumpled paper towel and keep warm while cooking the remainder. Serve warm with the dipping sauce.

PREPARATION TIME: 45 MINUTES   COOKING TIME: 15 MINUTES

NOTE: Nori, tonkatsu sauce and sake are available at Asian grocery stores and some supermarkets.

MARINATED SALMON STRIPS

2 sashimi-grade salmon fillets, each about
400 g (14 oz), skinned
4 cm (1¹/2 inch) piece fresh ginger, grated
1 garlic clove, finely chopped
3 spring onions (scallions), finely chopped
1 teaspoon sugar
2 tablespoons Japanese soy sauce
125 ml (4 fl oz/¹/2 cup) sake
pickled ginger, to garnish
pickled cucumber, to garnish

SERVES 4

Cut the salmon into thin strips and arrange them in a single layer in a large deep dish.

Put the ginger, garlic, spring onion, sugar, 1 teaspoon salt, soy sauce and sake in a small bowl and stir to combine. Pour the marinade over the salmon, cover and refrigerate for 1 hour.

Arrange the salmon, strip by strip, on a serving plate. Garnish with the pickled ginger and cucumber and serve chilled.

PREPARATION TIME: 15 MINUTES +   COOKING TIME: NIL

FISH TEMPURA

1 sheet nori (dried seaweed)
250 g (9 oz/2 cups) tempura flour,
plus 3 tablespoons
(see Notes, page 125)
250 ml (9 fl oz/1 cup) iced water
oil, for deep-frying
500 g (1 lb 2 oz) skinless fish fillets,
such as snapper, bream, haddock,
john dory or ling, cut into
bite-sized pieces
soy sauce, to serve

MAKES 24

Using scissors, cut the nori sheet into tiny squares and combine on a plate with 3 tablespoons of the tempura flour.

To make the tempura batter, quickly mix the iced water with the tempura flour. It should still be slightly lumpy. If it is too thick, add more water.

Fill a deep heavy-based saucepan one-third full of oil and heat to 180°C (350°F), or until a cube of bread dropped into the oil turns golden brown in 15 seconds. Make sure the oil stays at the same temperature and does not get too hot. The fish should cook through as well as brown.

Dip the fish pieces into the nori and flour, then in the tempura batter. Drain off the excess, then lower into the oil and deep-fry in batches until golden brown. Drain on crumpled paper towel. Season with salt and keep warm in a single layer on a baking tray in a 120°C (235°F/Gas ¹/2) oven. Serve immediately with soy sauce for dipping.

PREPARATION TIME: 15 MINUTES   COOKING TIME: 15 MINUTES

SALMON SUSHI ROLL

220 g (7³/4 oz/1 cup) Japanese
short-grain rice
1 tablespoon rice vinegar
2 teaspoons caster (superfine) sugar
125 g (4 oz) sashimi-grade salmon
1 small Lebanese (short) cucumber,
peeled
¹/2 small avocado
4 sheets roasted nori (dried seaweed),
20 x 18 cm (8 x 7 inches)
wasabi paste
3 tablespoons pickled ginger
Japanese soy sauce, to serve

MAKES ABOUT 30

Wash the rice under cold running water until the water runs clear, then drain thoroughly. Leave the rice in the strainer to drain for 1 hour. Put the rice in a saucepan and cover with 300 ml (10¹/2 fl oz) water. Cover the pan and bring the water to the boil, then reduce the heat to very low and simmer for 10 minutes. Remove the pan from the heat, remove the lid and put a clean cloth across the top to absorb excess moisture. Set aside for 10 minutes.

To make the sushi dressing, combine the vinegar, sugar and ¹/4 teaspoon salt in a small bowl.

Spread the rice over the base of a non-metallic dish or bowl, pour the sushi dressing over the top and use a rice paddle or spatula to mix the dressing through the rice. Fan the rice until it cools to room temperature. Cover with a damp cloth and set it aside, but do not refrigerate.

Using a very sharp knife, cut the fish into thin strips. Cut the cucumber and avocado into matchstick strips about 5 cm (2 inches) in length.

Put a nori sheet on a sushi mat, with the nori shiny side down and with the longest sides at the top and bottom. Top with a quarter of the rice, spreading it over the nori, leaving a 2 cm (³/4 inch) gap at the edge furthest away from you. Spread a very small amount of wasabi along the centre of the rice. Arrange a quarter of the pieces of fish, cucumber, avocado and ginger along the top of the wasabi. Starting with the end nearest to you, tightly roll up the mat and the nori, making sure you do not tuck the edge of the mat under the roll. When you have finished rolling, press the mat to make a round roll and press the nori edges together to seal. Repeat with the remaining ingredients.

Using a sharp knife, trim the ends and cut the rolls into 2.5 cm (1 inch) rounds. Serve the sushi with small bowls of soy sauce and extra wasabi — your guests can mix them together to their taste for a dipping sauce.

PREPARATION TIME: 45 MINUTES +   COOKING TIME: 15 MINUTES

NOTE: Sushi can be made up to 4 hours in advance and kept on a plate, covered with plastic wrap. Keep the large rolls intact and slice just before serving. Don't refrigerate or the rice will become hard.

SAVOURY EGG CUSTARD

200 g (7 oz) boneless, skinless chicken breasts, cut into bite-sized pieces
2 teaspoons sake
2 teaspoons Japanese soy sauce
2 leeks, white part only, sliced into matchsticks
1 small carrot, sliced into matchsticks
200 g (7 oz) English spinach, chopped

CUSTARD
1 litre (35 fl oz/4 cups) boiling water
80 g (2³⁄4 oz/1⁄2 cup) dashi granules
2 tablespoons Japanese soy sauce
6 eggs

SERVES 6

Divide the chicken pieces among six heatproof bowls. Combine the sake and soy sauce and pour over the chicken. Divide the leek, carrot and spinach among the bowls.

To make the custard, combine the boiling water and dashi granules in a heatproof bowl and stir to dissolve. Cool completely. Combine the dashi, soy sauce and eggs, and strain equal amounts into the bowls.

Fill a wok with 500 ml (17 fl oz/2 cups) water and bring to the boil. Cover the bowls with foil, place them in a steamer, then sit the steamer in the wok. Cover and cook over high heat for 20–30 minutes. Test the custard by inserting a fine skewer into the centre — it is cooked when the skewer comes out with no moisture clinging to it. Serve immediately.

PREPARATION TIME: 20 MINUTES   COOKING TIME: 30 MINUTES

PICKLED GINGER

500 g (1 lb 2 oz) young ginger
sea salt
500 ml (17 fl oz/2 cups) rice vinegar
170 g (6 oz/³⁄4 cup) caster (superfine) sugar

MAKES 500 G (1 LB 2 OZ)

Peel the ginger, then slice crossways into very thin slices. Put the ginger in a bowl with 1 teaspoon sea salt, toss together well and set aside for 10 minutes. Rinse under boiling water, then drain thoroughly.

Put the vinegar, sugar and 1¹⁄2 tablespoons sea salt into a small saucepan and cook over medium heat until the sugar has dissolved. Put the ginger in a sterilised 1 litre (35 fl oz/4 cup) jar, then pour on the vinegar mixture. Cover tightly and leave overnight before using. (The ginger won't be as pink as the commercial variety.) The pickled ginger will keep, stored in the refrigerator, for 2 months.

PREPARATION TIME: 20 MINUTES   COOKING TIME: 5 MINUTES

NIGIRI SUSHI

220 g (7³/4 oz/1 cup) Japanese
short-grain rice
1 tablespoon rice vinegar
2 teaspoons caster (superfine) sugar
300 g (10¹/2 oz) sashimi-grade salmon
or tuna
lemon juice
wasabi paste
nori (dried seaweed), cut into strips
(optional)

MAKES ABOUT 20

Wash the rice under cold running water until the water runs clear, then drain thoroughly. Leave the rice in the strainer to drain for 1 hour. Put the rice in a saucepan and cover with 300 ml (10¹/2 fl oz) water. Cover the pan and bring the water to the boil, then reduce the heat to very low and simmer for 10 minutes. Remove the pan from the heat, remove the lid and put a clean cloth across the top to absorb excess moisture. Set aside for 10 minutes.

To make the sushi dressing, combine the vinegar, sugar and ¹/4 teaspoon salt in a small bowl.

Spread the rice over the base of a non-metallic dish or bowl, pour the sushi dressing over the top and use a rice paddle or spatula to mix the dressing through the rice. Fan the rice until it cools to room temperature. Cover with a damp cloth and set it aside, but do not refrigerate.

Trim the fish into a neat rectangle, removing any blood or connective tissue. Using a sharp knife, cut paper-thin slices of fish from the trimmed fillet, cleaning your knife in a bowl of water and lemon juice after cutting each slice.

With wet hands, form 1 tablespoon of rice into an oval about the same length and width as your rectangles of fish. Place a piece of fish in the open palm of your left hand, then spread a small dab of wasabi over the centre of the fish. Place the rice oval on the fish and gently cup your palm to make a curve. Using the middle and index fingers of your right hand, press the rice onto the fish, firmly pushing. Turn over and repeat the shaping process, finishing with the fish on top of the rice. Serve with a strip of nori tied around the centre if desired.

PREPARATION TIME: 20 MINUTES +   COOKING TIME: 25 MINUTES

TONKATSU

500 g (1 lb 2 oz) pork schnitzels, trimmed of sinew

60 g (2¼ oz/½ cup) plain (all-purpose) flour

5 egg yolks

120 g (4¼ oz/2 cups) Japanese breadcrumbs (panko)

1 sheet nori (dried seaweed)

oil, for shallow-frying

250 ml (9 fl oz/1 cup) tonkatsu sauce

MAKES 40–50 SLICES

Sprinkle the pork with a good pinch each of salt and pepper, and lightly coat with the flour.

Beat the egg yolks with 2 tablespoons water. Dip each schnitzel in the egg, then in the breadcrumbs, pressing them on to ensure an even coating. Refrigerate the pork in a single layer on a plate, uncovered, for at least 2 hours.

Using a sharp knife, shred the nori very finely and then break into strips about 4 cm (1½ inches) long. Set aside until serving time.

Heat 2 cm (¾ inch) oil in a deep heavy-based saucepan to 180°C (350°F), or until a cube of bread dropped into the oil turns golden brown in 15 seconds. Cook two or three schnitzels at a time until golden brown on both sides, then drain on crumpled paper towel. Repeat the process with the remaining schnitzels.

Slice the schnitzels into 1 cm (½ inch) strips and reassemble into the original shape. Sprinkle with the nori strips and serve with tonkatsu sauce.

PREPARATION TIME: 35 MINUTES +   COOKING TIME: 15 MINUTES

NORI-WRAPPED FRIED MUSHROOMS

DIPPING SAUCE
80 ml (2$\frac{1}{2}$ fl oz/$\frac{1}{3}$ cup) Japanese soy sauce
100 ml (3$\frac{1}{2}$ fl oz) mirin
2 teaspoons grated fresh ginger
2 teaspoons sugar

3 sheets nori (dried seaweed), toasted
12 open-cup mushrooms, stalks removed
400 g (14 oz) orange sweet potato, peeled
oil, for deep-frying
220 ml (7$\frac{1}{2}$ fl oz) chilled soda water
1 egg, lightly beaten
125 g (4$\frac{1}{2}$ oz/1 cup) tempura flour
2 tablespoons wasabi powder

SERVES 4

To make the dipping sauce, put the soy sauce, mirin, ginger, sugar and 1 tablespoon water in a saucepan and cook, stirring constantly, over medium heat until the sugar has dissolved. Cover and keep warm.

Cut the nori sheets into twelve 4 cm (1$\frac{1}{2}$ inch) wide strips with scissors. Wrap a strip around each mushroom, dampening the end to help it stick. Cut the sweet potato into ribbon strips with a vegetable peeler.

Fill a wok one-third full of oil and heat to 190°C (375°F), or until a cube of bread dropped into the oil browns in 10 seconds. Cook the sweet potato in batches for 30–60 seconds, or until golden and crispy. Drain on crumpled paper towel, season and keep warm.

Put the soda water and egg in a large bowl and whisk well. Add the tempura flour and wasabi powder and loosely mix in with chopsticks or a fork until just combined — the batter should still be lumpy. Coat the mushrooms in the batter and cook in batches in the hot oil for 1–2 minutes, or until golden and crisp, turning once. Drain on crumpled paper towel and season with salt. Serve immediately with the sweet potato ribbons and the dipping sauce.

PREPARATION TIME: 30 MINUTES   COOKING TIME: 15 MINUTES

SKEWERS OF BEEF, CAPSICUM AND SPRING ONION

60 ml (2 fl oz/¼ cup) Japanese soy sauce
2 tablespoons mirin
2 teaspoons sesame oil
1 teaspoon sugar
2 tablespoons Japanese white sesame seeds
350 g (12 oz) scotch fillet, cut into bite-sized cubes
1 green capsicum (pepper), cut into small bite-sized pieces
6 spring onions (scallions), white part only, cut into short lengths
oil, for shallow-frying
2 eggs, beaten
60 g (2¼ oz/½ cup) plain (all-purpose) flour

MAKES 12

Soak 12 small wooden skewers in water for 30 minutes to ensure they don't burn during cooking.

Put the soy sauce, mirin, sesame oil, sugar and half the sesame seeds in a large bowl. Add the beef to the marinade, toss to combine, and marinate for 20 minutes. Drain the beef and gently pat dry with paper towel. Thread a piece of meat, capsicum and spring onion onto each skewer, repeating this pattern once more.

Heat 1 cm (½ inch) oil in a deep heavy-based frying pan until hot. Roll each skewer in the beaten egg, then lightly coat it in the flour. Add the skewers to the pan in two or three batches and fry until golden brown, turning each skewer regularly. Sprinkle over the remaining sesame seeds and serve immediately.

PREPARATION TIME: 40 MINUTES +   COOKING TIME: 20 MINUTES

MUSHROOMS WITH SESAME SEEDS

400 g (14 oz) flat mushrooms or shiitake mushrooms
2 tablespoons teriyaki sauce
2 tablespoons mirin
1 tablespoon sugar
1 tablespoon finely snipped chives
1 teaspoon sesame oil
1 tablespoon sesame seeds, toasted
10 chives, cut into short lengths

MAKES 30–35

Wipe the mushrooms with a damp cloth and discard the stalks. Put the mushrooms in a shallow dish. Combine the teriyaki sauce, mirin, sugar, snipped chives and sesame oil, pour over the mushrooms and leave for 5 minutes.

Put the mushrooms on a greased baking tray. Preheat the grill (broiler) to hot. Brush the mushrooms with half the marinade and grill (broil) for 5 minutes. Turn the mushrooms over, brush with the remaining marinade and grill for another 5 minutes, or until browned. Garnish with the sesame seeds and chives.

PREPARATION TIME: 15 MINUTES   COOKING TIME: 10 MINUTES

Skewers of beef, capsicum and spring onion

SUKIYAKI

500 g (1 lb 2 oz) scotch fillet, partially frozen

3 small white onions, each cut into 6 wedges

5 spring onions (scallions), white part only, cut into 4 cm (1½ inch) lengths

1 large carrot, cut into 4 cm (1½ inch) matchsticks

400 g (14 oz) small button mushrooms, stalks discarded, caps halved

½ small Chinese cabbage, cut into bite-sized pieces

180 g (6½ oz/2 cups) bean sprouts, trimmed

225 g (8 oz) tinned bamboo shoots, drained, trimmed into even-sized pieces

100 g (3½ oz) firm tofu, cut into 2 cm (¾ inch) cubes

100 g (3½ oz) fresh shirataki noodles

60 ml (2 fl oz/¼ cup) oil

6 eggs

SAUCE

80 ml (2½ fl oz/⅓ cup) Japanese soy sauce

60 ml (2 fl oz/¼ cup) beef stock

60 ml (2 fl oz/¼ cup) sake

60 ml (2 fl oz/¼ cup) mirin

2 tablespoons caster (superfine) sugar

SERVES 6

Using a very sharp knife, slice the partially frozen beef as thinly as possible, then arrange the slices on a large tray or platter, leaving room for the vegetables, tofu and noodles. Cover the beef and refrigerate the platter while preparing the remaining ingredients.

Arrange the prepared vegetables and tofu on the platter with the beef.

Cook the noodles in a saucepan of boiling water for about 3 minutes, or until just soft; do not overcook them or they will fall apart. Drain thoroughly and, if you like, use scissors to cut the cooked noodles into shorter lengths that can be picked up easily with chopsticks. Arrange the noodles on the platter with the meat and vegetables.

To make the sauce, combine the soy sauce, stock, sake, mirin and sugar in a small bowl and stir until the sugar dissolves.

Set the table with individual place settings, each with a serving bowl, a bowl of rice (see Note), a bowl to break an egg into, chopsticks and napkins. Place an electric frying pan on the table so it is within easy reach of each diner.

When all the diners are seated, heat the frying pan and brush it lightly with a little of the oil. When the pan is very hot, take about a third of each of the vegetables and cook them quickly for about 2 minutes, tossing constantly. Push the vegetables to the side of the pan. Add about a third of the beef in one layer and sear the slices for 30 seconds on each side, taking care not to overcook them. Drizzle a little of the sauce over the meat. Add some of the noodles and tofu to the pan and gently toss with the other ingredients.

Each diner breaks an egg into their bowl and whisks it with chopsticks. Mouthfuls of sukiyaki are then selected from the hot pan, dipped into the egg and eaten. When the diners are ready for more, the pan is reheated and the cooking process repeated.

PREPARATION TIME: 1 HOUR   COOKING TIME: 15 MINUTES

NOTE: Some people prefer to have sukiyaki on rice but it is not traditionally served with rice.

TAPAS TO MEZE

MEATBALLS IN SPICY TOMATO SAUCE

175 g (6 oz) minced (ground) pork
175 g (6 oz) minced (ground) veal
3 garlic cloves, crushed
35 g (1¼ oz/⅓ cup) dry breadcrumbs
1 teaspoon ground coriander
1 teaspoon ground nutmeg
1 teaspoon ground cumin
pinch ground cinnamon
1 egg
2 tablespoons olive oil

SPICY TOMATO SAUCE
1 tablespoon olive oil
1 onion, chopped
2 garlic cloves, crushed
125 ml (4 fl oz/½ cup) dry white wine
400 g (14 oz) tinned crushed tomatoes
1 tablespoon tomato paste
(concentrated purée)
125 ml (4 fl oz/½ cup) chicken stock
½ teaspoon cayenne pepper
80 g (2¾ oz/½ cup) frozen peas

SERVES 6

Combine the pork, veal, garlic, breadcrumbs, spices, egg and some salt and pepper in a bowl. Mix by hand until smooth and leaving the side of the bowl. Refrigerate, covered, for 30 minutes.

Roll tablespoons of the mixture into balls. Heat 1 tablespoon of the oil in a frying pan over medium-high heat and cook half the meatballs for 2–3 minutes, turning frequently, until browned. Remove and drain on paper towel. Add the remaining oil, if necessary, and brown the rest of the meatballs. Drain on paper towel.

To make the spicy tomato sauce, heat the oil in a frying pan over medium heat and cook the onion, stirring occasionally, for 3 minutes, or until transparent. Add the garlic and cook for 1 minute, then increase the heat to high, add the wine and boil for 1 minute. Add the tomato, tomato paste and stock and simmer for 10 minutes. Add the cayenne pepper, peas and meatballs. Simmer for 5–10 minutes, or until the sauce is thick and the meatballs are cooked through. Serve with crusty bread.

PREPARATION TIME: 40 MINUTES +   COOKING TIME: 30 MINUTES

OLIVES WITH HERBS DE PROVENCE

500 g (1 lb 2 oz) niçoise or ligurian olives
1 garlic clove, crushed
2 teaspoons chopped basil
1 teaspoon chopped thyme
1 teaspoon chopped rosemary
1 teaspoon chopped marjoram
1 teaspoon chopped oregano
1 teaspoon chopped mint
1 teaspoon fennel seeds
2 tablespoons lemon juice
125 ml (4 fl oz/½ cup) olive oil
olive oil, extra

MAKES 500 G (1 LB 2 OZ)

Rinse and drain the olives and put in a bowl. Combine the garlic, fresh herbs, fennel seeds, lemon juice and olive oil and pour over the olives. Stir to mix well.

Layer the olives and marinade in a wide-necked, 750 ml (26 fl oz/3 cup) sterilised jar, adding extra olive oil to cover the olives. Seal and marinate in the refrigerator for at least 1 week before using. Serve the olives at room temperature.

PREPARATION TIME: 20 MINUTES +   COOKING TIME: NIL

NOTE: To sterilise jars, wash the jar and lid in hot soapy water, rinse well in hot water and then dry in a 120°C (235°F/Gas ½) oven for 20 minutes. Do not dry with a tea towel.

MIXED OLIVE PICKLES

200 g (7 oz) jumbo green olives
4 gherkins (pickles), thickly sliced diagonally
1 tablespoon capers
2 small brown onions, quartered
2 teaspoons mustard seeds
1 tablespoon dill sprigs
125 ml (4 fl oz/½ cup) tarragon vinegar
about 125 ml (4 fl oz/½ cup) olive oil

MAKES ABOUT 250 G (9 OZ)

Combine the green olives, gherkins, capers, onion, mustard seeds and dill sprigs in a bowl.

Spoon into a 500 ml (17 fl oz/2 cup) sterilised jar and pour in the tarragon vinegar. Top up with the olive oil, using enough oil to ensure the olives are covered completely. Seal and refrigerate for at least 2 days before using. Shake the jar occasionally. Serve the olives at room temperature.

PREPARATION TIME: 15 MINUTES +   COOKING TIME: NIL

STUFFED SQUID

TOMATO SAUCE

4 large ripe tomatoes

1 tablespoon olive oil

1 onion, finely chopped

1 garlic clove, crushed

60 ml (2 fl oz/1/4 cup) red wine

1 tablespoon chopped oregano

RICE STUFFING

1 tablespoon olive oil

2 spring onions (scallions), chopped

280 g (10 oz/1 1/2 cups) cold, cooked rice (see Notes)

60 g (2 1/4 oz) pine nuts

75 g (2 1/2 oz/1/2 cup) currants

2 tablespoons chopped flat-leaf (Italian) parsley

2 teaspoons finely grated lemon zest

1 egg, lightly beaten

1 kg (2 lb 4 oz) squid tubes

SERVES 4   PREPARATION TIME: 40 MINUTES   COOKING TIME: 35 MINUTES

Preheat the oven to 160°C (315°F/Gas 2–3). To make the tomato sauce, score a cross in the base of each tomato. Put the tomatoes in a heatproof bowl and cover with boiling water. Leave for 30 seconds, then transfer to cold water, drain and peel the skin away from the cross. Cut the tomatoes in half and roughly chop the flesh.

Heat the olive oil in a frying pan. Add the onion and garlic and cook over low heat for about 2 minutes, stirring frequently, until the onion is soft. Add the tomato, wine and oregano and bring to the boil. Reduce the heat, then cover and cook over low heat for 10 minutes.

Meanwhile, to make the rice stuffing, mix all the ingredients except the egg in a bowl. Add enough egg to moisten the ingredients.

Wash the squid and pat dry with paper towel. Remove the quill and any skin. Three-quarters fill each tube with the stuffing and secure the ends with toothpicks or skewers. Place in a single layer in an ovenproof dish.

Pour the tomato sauce over the squid, cover the dish and bake for 20 minutes, or until the squid are tender. Cut the squid into thick slices. Spoon the sauce over just before serving.

NOTES: You will need to cook 100 g (3 1/2 oz/1/2 cup) rice for this recipe.

The cooking time for the squid will depend on their size. Choose small squid because they will be more tender.

GARLIC MUSHROOMS

6 garlic cloves
1½ tablespoons lemon juice
650 g (1 lb 7 oz) button mushrooms, sliced (see Note)
60 ml (2 fl oz/¼ cup) olive oil
¼ small red chilli, finely chopped
2 teaspoons chopped flat-leaf (Italian) parsley

SERVES 4

Crush four of the garlic cloves and thinly slice the rest. Sprinkle the lemon juice over the sliced mushrooms.

Heat the olive oil in a large frying pan and add the crushed garlic and chilli. Stir over medium–high heat for 10 seconds, then add the mushrooms. Season with salt and pepper and cook, stirring often, for 8-10 minutes. Stir in the sliced garlic and parsley and cook for another minute. Serve hot.

PREPARATION TIME: 10 MINUTES   COOKING TIME: 10 MINUTES

NOTE: You can also use field, Swiss brown or any wild mushrooms for this recipe, but take care to adjust the cooking times if you use the more fragile wild mushrooms.

TZATZIKI

2 Lebanese (short) cucumbers (about 300 g/10½ oz)
400 g (14 oz) Greek-style yoghurt
4 garlic cloves, crushed
3 tablespoons finely chopped mint
1 tablespoon lemon juice
chopped mint, extra, to serve

SERVES 6–8

Cut the cucumbers in half lengthways, scoop out the seeds with a teaspoon and discard. Leave the skin on and coarsely grate the cucumber into a small colander, sprinkle with salt and set the colander over a large bowl or the sink for 15 minutes to drain off any bitter juices.

Meanwhile, combine the yoghurt, garlic, mint and lemon juice in a bowl.

Rinse the cucumber under cold water then, taking small handfuls, squeeze out any excess moisture. Stir the cucumber into the yoghurt and season with salt and pepper. Scatter with the extra mint before serving, or cover and refrigerate until needed. Serve as a dip with bread or as a sauce for seafood or meats.

PREPARATION TIME: 10 MINUTES +   COOKING TIME: NIL

CHICKEN AND CHORIZO PAELLA

1/4 teaspoon saffron threads
60 ml (2 fl oz/1/4 cup) olive oil
1 large red capsicum (pepper), seeded and cut into 5 mm (1/4 inch) strips
600 g (1 lb 5 oz) boneless, skinless chicken thighs, cut into 3 cm (1 1/4 inch) cubes
200 g (7 oz) chorizo sausage, cut into 2 cm (3/4 inch) slices
200 g (7 oz) mushrooms, thinly sliced
3 garlic cloves, crushed
1 tablespoon finely grated lemon zest
700 g (1 lb 9 oz) ripe tomatoes, roughly chopped
200 g (7 oz) green beans, cut into 3 cm (1 1/4 inch) lengths
1 tablespoon chopped rosemary
2 tablespoons chopped flat-leaf (Italian) parsley
440 g (15 1/2 oz/2 cups) short-grain rice
750 ml (26 fl oz/3 cups) hot chicken stock
lemon wedges, to serve

SERVES 6

Put the saffron in a bowl and pour over 60 ml (2 fl oz/1/4 cup) hot water. Set aside to infuse.

Heat the olive oil in a paella pan or in a large, deep heavy-based frying pan over medium heat. Add the capsicum and cook, stirring, for about 6 minutes, or until softened, then remove from the pan.

Add the chicken to the pan and cook for 10 minutes, or until brown on all sides. Remove from the pan. Add the chorizo and cook for 5 minutes, or until golden on all sides. Remove from the pan. Add the mushrooms, garlic and lemon zest and cook for 5 minutes. Stir in the tomato and capsicum and cook for another 5 minutes, or until the tomato is soft.

Add the beans, rosemary, parsley, saffron mixture, rice, chicken and chorizo. Stir briefly and then add the hot stock. Do not stir at this point. Reduce the heat to low and simmer for 30 minutes. Remove from the heat, cover and leave to stand for 10 minutes. Serve the paella with lemon wedges.

PREPARATION TIME: 30 MINUTES   COOKING TIME: 1 HOUR

NOTE: Paella pans are available from some specialist kitchenware shops.

CRISPY POTATOES IN SPICY TOMATO SAUCE

1 kg (2 lb 4 oz) all-purpose potatoes, such as desiree
oil, for deep-frying
500 g (1 lb 2 oz) ripe roma (plum) tomatoes
2 tablespoons olive oil
¼ red onion, finely chopped
2 garlic cloves, crushed
3 teaspoons paprika
¼ teaspoon cayenne pepper
1 bay leaf
1 teaspoon sugar
1 tablespoon chopped flat-leaf (Italian) parsley, to garnish

SERVES 6

Cut the potatoes into 2 cm (³/₄ inch) cubes. Rinse, then drain well and pat completely dry.

Fill a large heavy-based saucepan or deep-fryer one-third full of oil and heat to 180°C (350°F), or until a cube of bread dropped into the oil turns golden brown in 15 seconds. Cook the potato in batches for 10 minutes, or until golden. Drain well on paper towel. Do not discard the oil.

Score a cross in the base of each tomato. Put the tomatoes in a heatproof bowl and cover with boiling water. Leave for 30 seconds, then transfer to cold water, drain and peel the skin away from the cross. Cut the tomatoes in half and roughly chop the flesh.

Heat the olive oil in a saucepan over medium heat and cook the onion for 3 minutes, or until softened. Add the garlic, paprika and cayenne pepper and cook for 1–2 minutes, until fragrant.

Add the tomato, bay leaf, sugar and 90 ml (3 fl oz) water and cook, stirring occasionally, for 20 minutes, or until thick and pulpy. Cool slightly and remove the bay leaf. Transfer the tomato mixture to a food processor and blend until smooth, adding a little water if necessary. Before you are ready to serve, return the sauce to the saucepan and simmer over low heat for 2 minutes to heat through. Season well.

Reheat the oil to 180°C (350°F) and cook the potato again, in batches, for 2 minutes, or until very crisp and golden. Drain on paper towel. This second frying makes the potato extra crispy and stops the sauce soaking in immediately. Place on a platter and cover with the warmed tomato sauce. Sprinkle with parsley and serve.

PREPARATION TIME: 15 MINUTES   COOKING TIME: 1 HOUR

HAM AND OLIVE
EMPANDILLAS

2 hard-boiled eggs, roughly chopped
40 g (1^1/2 oz) stuffed green olives,
chopped
95 g (3^1/4 oz) ham, finely chopped
30 g (1 oz/^{1}/4 cup) grated cheddar cheese
3 sheets ready-rolled puff pastry
1 egg yolk, lightly beaten

MAKES ABOUT 15

Preheat the oven to 220°C (425°F/Gas 7). Lightly grease two baking trays.

Combine the boiled eggs with the olives, ham and cheese in a bowl. Cut the puff pastry sheets into 10 cm (4 inch) rounds (about five rounds from each sheet). Spoon a tablespoon of the ham and olive mixture into the centre of each round, fold over the pastry to enclose the filling and crimp the edges to seal.

Place the pastries on the trays, spacing them 2 cm (^{3}/4 inch) apart. Brush with the egg yolk and bake for 15 minutes, or until brown and puffed, swapping the trays around in the oven after 10 minutes. Cover loosely with foil if browning too much. Serve hot.

PREPARATION TIME: 45 MINUTES   COOKING TIME: 15 MINUTES

FETA AND MINT SPREAD

175 g (6 oz) crumbled feta cheese
100 g (3½ oz) ricotta cheese
60 ml (2 fl oz/¼ cup) olive oil
1 large handful mint, chopped
crusty bread, to serve

SERVES 4–6

Combine the feta, ricotta and olive oil in a bowl and mash with a fork until well combined. The mixture should still contain a few small lumps of cheese.

Add the mint and some freshly ground black pepper. Lightly toast the bread and serve topped with the feta spread.

PREPARATION TIME: 10 MINUTES   COOKING TIME: NIL

NOTES: These could be topped with slices of roasted tomato or capsicum (pepper).

Store in an airtight container in the refrigerator for up to 5 days.

SPLIT PEA PURÉE

60 ml (2 fl oz/¼ cup) olive oil
1 onion, finely chopped
330 g (11½ oz/1½ cups) dried yellow
split peas, rinsed
1–2 tablespoons lemon juice
2 tablespoons baby capers, rinsed,
to garnish
60 g (2¼ oz) feta cheese, crumbled,
to garnish
2 tablespoons extra virgin olive oil,
to serve
1 lemon, cut into small wedges, to serve

SERVES 4–6

Heat the olive oil in a large heavy-based saucepan over medium heat and cook the onion for 5 minutes, or until softened.

Add the split peas and 1.25 litres (44 fl oz/5 cups) water to the saucepan and bring to the boil. Reduce the heat, then cover and simmer for 45–50 minutes, or until the peas are very tender and falling apart. Stir frequently during cooking to prevent the split peas catching on the base of the saucepan. Uncover and cook for a further 15–20 minutes, or until the mixture has reduced and thickened. Season with salt and pepper, to taste, and stir in the lemon juice.

Serve warm or at room temperature, garnished with capers and crumbled feta. Drizzle the olive oil over the top and serve with lemon wedges and crusty bread.

PREPARATION TIME: 10 MINUTES   COOKING TIME: 1 HOUR 15 MINUTES

Feta and mint spread

OCTOPUS IN RED WINE STEW

1 kg (2 lb 4 oz) baby octopus
2 tablespoons olive oil
1 large onion, chopped
3 garlic cloves, crushed
1 bay leaf
750 ml (26 fl oz/3 cups) red wine
60 ml (2 fl oz/¼ cup) red wine vinegar
400 g (14 oz) tinned crushed tomatoes
1 tablespoon tomato paste
(concentrated purée)
1 tablespoon finely chopped oregano
¼ teaspoon ground cinnamon
small pinch ground cloves
1 teaspoon sugar
2 tablespoons chopped flat-leaf (Italian)
parsley

SERVES 4–6

To prepare each octopus, using a small knife, cut between the head and tentacles, just below the eyes. Grasp the body and push the beak out and up through the centre of the tentacles with your fingers. Cut the eyes from the head by slicing a small round off with a small sharp knife. Discard the eye section. Carefully slit through one side of the head and remove any gut from inside. Thoroughly rinse all the octopus under running water.

Heat the olive oil in a large saucepan, add the onion and cook over high heat for 5 minutes, or until starting to brown. Add the garlic and bay leaf and cook for another minute. Add the octopus and stir to thoroughly coat in the onion mixture.

Add the wine, vinegar, tomatoes, tomato paste, oregano, cinnamon, cloves and sugar. Bring to the boil, then reduce the heat to low and simmer for 1 hour, or until the octopus is tender and the sauce has thickened slightly. Stir in the parsley and season.

PREPARATION TIME: 20 MINUTES   COOKING TIME: 1 HOUR 10 MINUTES

NOTE: The cooking time for octopus varies according to their size. Generally the smaller octopus are not as tough as the larger ones and will take less time to cook.

GREEN BEANS WITH TOMATO AND OLIVE OIL

80 ml (2½ fl oz/⅓ cup) olive oil
1 large onion, chopped
3 garlic cloves, finely chopped
400 g (14 oz) tinned chopped tomatoes
½ teaspoon sugar
750 g (1 lb 10 oz) green beans, trimmed
3 tablespoons chopped flat-leaf (Italian) parsley

SERVES 4

Heat the olive oil in a large frying pan, add the onion and cook over medium heat for 4–5 minutes, until softened. Add the garlic and cook for another 30 seconds.

Add the tomatoes, sugar and 125 ml (4 fl oz/½ cup) water, then season with salt and pepper. Bring to the boil, then reduce the heat and simmer for 10 minutes, or until reduced slightly.

Add the beans and simmer for another 10 minutes, or until the beans are tender and the tomato mixture is pulpy. Stir in the parsley. Check the seasoning, and adjust according to your taste. Serve immediately, as a side dish.

PREPARATION TIME: 10 MINUTES   COOKING TIME: 25 MINUTES

PROVENÇAL ROAST TOMATOES

60 g (2¼ oz/¾ cup) fresh breadcrumbs
2 tablespoons chopped flat-leaf (Italian) parsley
2 tablespoons chopped basil
1 tablespoon chopped oregano
4 large vine-ripened tomatoes
4–6 garlic cloves, finely chopped
2 tablespoons olive oil

SERVES 4

Preheat the oven to 180°C (350°F/Gas 4). Combine the breadcrumbs and herbs in a bowl and season with salt and pepper.

Halve each tomato horizontally and scoop out the core and seeds with a teaspoon.

Sprinkle some garlic into each tomato half, then top with the breadcrumb mixture. Drizzle with olive oil and bake for 40 minutes, or until soft. Serve as a side dish.

PREPARATION TIME: 10 MINUTES   COOKING TIME: 40 MINUTES

Green beans with tomato and olive oil

SPANISH BAKED EGGS

500 g (1 lb 2 oz) ripe tomatoes
60 ml (2 fl oz/¼ cup) olive oil
400 g (14 oz) all-purpose potatoes,
cut into 2 cm (³/₄ inch) cubes
1 red capsicum (pepper), cut into strips
1 onion, chopped
100 g (3½ oz) serrano ham (or thickly
sliced soft, pale prosciutto)
150 g (5½ oz) thin asparagus spears,
trimmed
100 g (3½ oz/²/₃ cup) fresh or frozen
green peas
100 g (3½ oz) baby green beans,
trimmed and sliced
2 tablespoons tomato paste
(concentrated purée)
4 eggs
100 g (3½ oz) chorizo sausage,
thinly sliced
2 tablespoons chopped flat-leaf
(Italian) parsley

SERVES 4

Score a cross in the base of each tomato. Put the tomatoes in a heatproof bowl and cover with boiling water. Leave for 30 seconds, then transfer to cold water, drain and peel the skin away from the cross. Cut the tomatoes in half and roughly chop.

Heat the olive oil in a large frying pan and sauté the potato over medium heat for 8 minutes, or until golden. Remove with a slotted spoon. Lower the heat and add the capsicum and onion to the pan. Slice two of the ham slices into pieces similar in size to the capsicum and add to the pan. Fry for 6 minutes, or until the onion is soft.

Reserve four asparagus spears. Add the rest to the pan with the peas, beans, tomato and tomato paste. Stir in 125 ml (4 fl oz/½ cup) water and season well with salt and pepper. Return the potato to the pan. Cover and cook over low heat for 10 minutes, stirring occasionally.

Preheat the oven to 180°C (350°F/Gas 4). Grease a large oval ovenproof dish. Transfer the vegetables to the dish, without any excess liquid. Using the back of a spoon, make four evenly spaced deep indentations in the vegetables and break an egg into each. Top with the reserved asparagus and the chorizo. Slice the remaining ham into large pieces and distribute over the top. Sprinkle with the parsley. Bake for 20 minutes, or until the egg whites are just set. Serve warm.

PREPARATION TIME: 20 MINUTES   COOKING TIME: 50 MINUTES

POTATO AND ANCHOVY SALAD

1 kg (2 lb 4 oz) waxy potatoes, such as pink fir apple, binji or kipfler (fingerling), unpeeled
60 ml (2 fl oz/¼ cup) dry white wine
1 tablespoon cider vinegar
60 ml (2 fl oz/¼ cup) olive oil
4 spring onions (scallions), finely chopped
35 g (1¼ oz) drained anchovy fillets,
1 tablespoon chopped flat-leaf (Italian) parsley
1 tablespoon snipped chives

SERVES 6

Cook the potatoes in their skins in boiling salted water for 20 minutes, or until just tender. Drain and peel away the skins while the potatoes are still warm. Cut into 1 cm (½ inch) thick slices.

Put the wine, vinegar, olive oil and spring onion in a large heavy-based frying pan over low heat and add the potato slices. Shake the pan to coat the potatoes, then reheat gently.

When hot, remove from the heat and season with salt and pepper. Roughly chop half the anchovies and toss them through the potatoes along with the parsley and chives. Transfer to a platter and put the remaining anchovies on top. Serve warm or at room temperature.

PREPARATION TIME: 20 MINUTES COOKING TIME: 25 MINUTES

ROASTED RED CAPSICUMS

8 red capsicums (peppers)
2 garlic cloves, crushed
80 ml (2½ fl oz/⅓ cup) red wine vinegar
2 teaspoons thyme

SERVES 4–6

Cut the capsicums into quarters, then remove the seeds and membrane. Put the capsicum quarters, skin side up, under a hot grill (broiler). Cook until the skin blackens and blisters. Remove from the grill and put in a plastic bag until cool, then peel off the skin. Slice the flesh into 3 cm (1¼ inch) wide strips. Place the strips in a clean bowl.

Combine the garlic and vinegar in a small bowl and season with salt. Pour the dressing over the capsicum and gently toss to coat. Sprinkle the thyme over the top and refrigerate for at least 4 hours. Serve the capsicums at room temperature as a side dish.

PREPARATION TIME: 10 MINUTES + COOKING TIME: 10 MINUTES

Potato and anchovy salad

SALT COD FRITTERS

500 g (1 lb 2 oz) salt cod
1 large all-purpose potato (200 g/7 oz),
unpeeled
2 tablespoons milk
60 ml (2 fl oz/¼ cup) olive oil
1 small onion, finely chopped
2 garlic cloves, crushed
30 g (1 oz/¼ cup) self-raising flour
2 eggs, separated
1 tablespoon chopped flat-leaf
(Italian) parsley
olive oil, extra, for deep-frying
lemon wedges, to serve

MAKES 35

Soak the cod in cold water for 24 hours, changing the water regularly to remove as much salt as possible. Cook the potato in a saucepan of boiling water for 20 minutes, or until soft. When cool, peel and mash with the milk and 2 tablespoons of the olive oil.

Drain the cod, cut into large pieces and place in a saucepan. Cover with water, bring to the boil over high heat, then reduce the heat to medium and cook for 10 minutes, or until the cod is soft and there is a froth on the surface. Drain. When cool enough to handle, remove the skin and any bones from the cod, then mash well with a fork until flaky.

Heat the remaining olive oil in a small frying pan over medium heat and cook the onion for 5 minutes, or until softened and starting to brown. Add the garlic and cook for 1 minute. Remove from the heat.

Combine the mashed potato, cod, onion and garlic, flour, egg yolks and parsley in a bowl and season with salt and pepper. Whisk the egg whites until stiff, then fold into the potato and cod mixture.

Fill a large heavy-based saucepan one-third full of olive oil and heat to 190°C (375°F), or until a cube of bread dropped into the oil turns golden brown in 10 seconds. Drop heaped tablespoons of mixture into the oil and cook for 2 minutes, or until puffed and golden. Drain and serve with lemon wedges.

PREPARATION TIME: 20 MINUTES +   COOKING TIME: 1 HOUR

PAPRIKA GARLIC CHICKEN

1 kg (2 lb 4 oz) boneless, skinless chicken thighs
1 tablespoon paprika
2 tablespoons olive oil
8 garlic cloves, unpeeled
60 ml (2 fl oz/¼ cup) brandy
125 ml (4 fl oz/½ cup) chicken stock
1 bay leaf
2 tablespoons chopped flat-leaf (Italian) parsley

SERVES 6

Trim any excess fat from the chicken and cut the thighs into thirds. Combine the paprika with some salt and pepper in a bowl, add the chicken and toss to coat.

Heat half the olive oil in a large frying pan over medium heat and cook the garlic for 1–2 minutes, until brown. Remove from the pan. Increase the heat to high and cook the chicken in batches for 5 minutes each batch, or until brown. Return all the chicken to the pan, add the brandy and boil for 30 seconds, then add the stock and bay leaf. Reduce the heat, cover and simmer over low heat for 10 minutes.

Meanwhile, peel the garlic and put it in a mortar or small bowl. Add the parsley and pound with the pestle or crush with a fork to form a paste. Stir into the chicken, then cover and cook for 10 minutes, or until tender. Serve hot.

PREPARATION TIME: 20 MINUTES   COOKING TIME: 35 MINUTES

LEMONY CHICKEN

60 ml (2 fl oz/¼ cup) olive oil
1 kg (2 lb 4 oz) chicken drumsticks, seasoned
1 large leek, halved lengthways, washed and thinly sliced
4 large strips lemon zest, white pith removed
125 ml (4 fl oz/½ cup) lemon juice
250 ml (9 fl oz/1 cup) dry white wine
500 g (1 lb 2 oz) baby carrots, trimmed

SERVES 4

Heat the olive oil in a large heavy-based frying pan. Add the chicken in two batches and sauté for 6–8 minutes, or until brown and crispy. Return all the chicken to the pan, add the leek and cook until the leek is just wilted. Add the strips of lemon zest and cook for 1–2 minutes.

Pour the lemon juice and wine into the pan and allow the flavours to combine for a few seconds. Stir, add the carrots, then cover and cook for 30–35 minutes, stirring occasionally, until the chicken is cooked through. Remove the lemon zest, then taste and adjust the seasoning if necessary.

PREPARATION TIME: 10 MINUTES   COOKING TIME: 55 MINUTES

STUFFED MUSSELS

18 black mussels
2 teaspoons olive oil
2 spring onions (scallions), finely chopped
1 garlic clove, crushed
1 tablespoon tomato paste
(concentrated purée)
2 teaspoons lemon juice
3 tablespoons chopped flat-leaf
(Italian) parsley
35 g (1¼ oz/⅓ cup) dry breadcrumbs
2 eggs, beaten
oil, for deep-frying
lemon wedges, to serve

WHITE SAUCE
40 g (1½ oz) butter
30 g (1 oz/¼ cup) plain (all-purpose) flour
80 ml (2½ fl oz/⅓ cup) milk

MAKES 18

Scrub the mussels and remove the hairy beards. Discard any open mussels or those that don't close when tapped on the work surface. Bring 250 ml (9 fl oz/1 cup) water to the boil in a saucepan, add the mussels, cover and cook for 3–4 minutes, shaking the pan occasionally, until the mussels have just opened. Remove them as soon as they open or they will be tough. Strain the liquid into a bowl until you have 80 ml (2½ fl oz/⅓ cup). Discard any unopened mussels. Remove the opened mussels from their shells and discard one half-shell from each. Finely chop the mussel meat.

Heat the olive oil in a large frying pan over medium heat, add the spring onion and cook for 1 minute. Add the garlic and cook for 1 minute. Stir in the mussel meat, tomato paste, lemon juice, 2 tablespoons of the parsley and season with salt and pepper. Set aside to cool.

To make the white sauce, melt the butter in a saucepan over low heat. Stir in the flour and cook for 1 minute, or until pale and foaming. Remove the pan from the heat and gradually whisk in the reserved mussel liquid, milk and some pepper. Return to the heat and boil, stirring, for 1 minute, or until the sauce thickens. Reduce the heat and simmer for 2 minutes. Set aside to cool.

Spoon the mussel mixture into the reserved half-shells. Top each with some of the white sauce and smooth the surface, making the mixture heaped. Combine the breadcrumbs and remaining parsley. Dip the mussels in the beaten egg, then press in the crumbs to cover the top.

Fill a deep heavy-based saucepan one-third full of oil and heat to 180°C (350°F), or until a cube of bread dropped into the oil turns golden brown in 15 seconds. Cook the mussels in batches for 2 minutes each batch. Remove with a slotted spoon and drain well. Serve the mussels hot with lemon wedges.

PREPARATION TIME: 40 MINUTES   COOKING TIME: 20 MINUTES

MEAT PATTIES WITH HALOUMI FILLING

8 slices white bread, crusts removed
700 g (1 lb 9 oz) minced (ground) lamb
or beef
1 tablespoon chopped flat-leaf
(Italian) parsley
3 tablespoons chopped mint
1 onion, grated
2 eggs, lightly beaten
140 g (5 oz) haloumi cheese (see Note)
30 g (1 oz/1/4 cup) plain (all-purpose) flour
olive oil, for shallow-frying

MAKES 24

Put the bread in a bowl, cover with water and then squeeze out as much water as possible. Put the bread in a bowl with the lamb or beef, parsley, mint, onion, egg and season with pepper and 1/2 teaspoon salt. Knead the mixture by hand for 2–3 minutes, breaking up the meat and any large pieces of bread with your fingers. The mixture should be smooth and leave the side of the bowl. Cover and refrigerate for 30 minutes.

Cut the haloumi into 24 rectangles, 3 x 1 x 1 cm (1 1/4 x 1/2 x 1/2 inch). Place the flour in a shallow dish. Divide the meat mixture into level tablespoon portions. Roll a portion into a long shape and flatten in the palm of your hand. Place the haloumi in the centre and top with another portion of meat mixture. Pinch the edges together and roll into a torpedo about 6 cm (2 1/2 inches) long. Repeat with the remaining meat and cheese.

Put 2 cm (3/4 inch) olive oil in a deep heavy-based frying pan and heat to 180°C (350°F), or until a cube of bread dropped into the oil turns golden brown in 15 seconds. Toss the meat patties in flour, shake off the excess and fry in batches for 3–5 minutes, or until brown and cooked through. Drain on crumpled paper towel. Serve hot.

PREPARATION TIME: 25 MINUTES +   COOKING TIME: 15 MINUTES

NOTE: Haloumi is a creamy white sheep's milk cheese kept in brine. It can be bought from delicatessens and supermarkets.

OCTOPUS IN GARLIC ALMOND SAUCE

1 kg (2 lb 4 oz) baby octopus
1/2 small red capsicum (pepper)
120 g (4 1/4 oz/1 1/3 cups) flaked almonds
3 garlic cloves, crushed
80 ml (2 1/2 fl oz/1/3 cup) red wine vinegar
185 ml (6 fl oz/3/4 cup) olive oil
125 ml (4 fl oz/1/2 cup) boiling water
2 tablespoons chopped flat-leaf (Italian) parsley

SERVES 4

Using a small knife, carefully cut between the head and tentacles of the octopus and push the beak out and up through the centre of the tentacles with your finger. Cut the eyes from the head of the octopus by slicing off a small disc with a sharp knife. Discard the eye section. To clean the octopus head, carefully slit through one side and rinse out the gut. Drop the octopus into a large pan of boiling water and simmer for 20–40 minutes, depending on size, until tender. After 15 minutes cooking, start pricking them with a skewer to test for tenderness. When ready, remove from the heat and cool in the pan for 15 minutes.

To make the sauce, cut the capsicum into quarters, then remove the seeds and membrane. Put the capsicum quarters, skin side up, under a hot grill (broiler). Cook until the skin blackens and blisters. Remove from the grill and put in a plastic bag until cool, then peel off the skin. Put the capsicum flesh in a food processor with the almonds and garlic, then purée. With the motor running, gradually pour in the vinegar followed by the olive oil. Stir in the boiling water and parsley. Season to taste with salt and pepper.

To serve, cut the octopus tentacles into pieces. Place in a serving bowl with the sauce and toss to coat. Serve warm, or chill and serve as a salad.

PREPARATION TIME: 25 MINUTES +   COOKING TIME: 50 MINUTES

TORTILLA

500 g (1 lb 2 oz) all-purpose potatoes,
cut into 1 cm (½ inch) slices
60 ml (2 fl oz/¼ cup) olive oil
1 onion, thinly sliced
4 garlic cloves, thinly sliced
2 tablespoons finely chopped flat-leaf
(Italian) parsley
6 eggs

SERVES 6–8

Put the potato slices in a large saucepan, cover with cold water and bring to the boil over high heat. Boil for 5 minutes, then drain and set aside.

Heat the olive oil in a deep non-stick frying pan over medium heat. Add the onion and garlic and cook for 5 minutes, or until the onion softens. Add the potato and parsley and stir to combine. Cook over medium heat for 5 minutes, gently pressing down into the pan.

Whisk the eggs with 1 teaspoon each of salt and pepper and pour evenly over the potato. Cover and cook over low–medium heat for 20 minutes, or until the eggs are just set. Slide onto a serving plate or serve directly from the pan.

PREPARATION TIME: 20 MINUTES   COOKING TIME: 35 MINUTES

FRIED SQUID

1 kg (2 lb 4 oz) small squid
oil, for deep-frying
plain (all-purpose) flour for coating,
well-seasoned
lemon wedges, to serve

SERVES 4

To clean the squid, gently pull the tentacles away from the hoods and remove the intestines and the transparent quills. Trim off the tentacles below the eyes and detach the beaks. Under cold running water, pull away the skin. Rinse the bodies and detach the side wings. Slice the bodies into 5 mm (¼ inch) rings. Pat dry the rings, wings and tentacles.

Heat the oil in a deep, heavy-based frying pan to 180°C (350°F), or until a cube of bread dropped into the oil turns golden brown in 15 seconds. Toss the squid in the seasoned flour and shake off any excess. Fry in batches, for 2–3 minutes each batch, or until golden. Serve the squid with lemon wedges.

PREPARATION TIME: 20 MINUTES   COOKING TIME: 15 MINUTES

MUSSELS SAGANAKI

750 g (1 lb 10 oz) black mussels
420 g (15 oz) ripe tomatoes
125 ml (4 fl oz/¹/₂ cup) dry white wine
3 thyme sprigs
1 bay leaf
1 tablespoon olive oil
1 large onion, finely chopped
1 garlic clove, finely chopped
2 tablespoons tomato paste
(concentrated purée)
¹/₂ teaspoon sugar
1 tablespoon red wine vinegar
70 g (2¹/₂ oz) Greek feta cheese,
crumbled
1 teaspoon thyme

SERVES 6

Scrub the mussels with a stiff brush and pull out the hairy beards. Discard any broken mussels, or open ones that don't close when tapped on the work surface. Rinse well.

To peel the tomatoes, score a cross in the base of each tomato. Put the tomatoes in a heatproof bowl and cover with boiling water. Leave for 30 seconds, then transfer to cold water, drain and peel the skin away from the cross. Cut the tomatoes in half and finely chop the flesh.

Put the wine, thyme sprigs and bay leaf in a large saucepan and bring to the boil. Add the mussels and cook for 4–5 minutes, or until just opened. Pour the mussel liquid through a strainer into a heatproof bowl and reserve. Discard any unopened mussels. Remove the top half-shell from each mussel and discard.

Heat the olive oil in a large saucepan, add the onion and stir over medium heat for 3 minutes. Add the garlic and cook for 1 minute, or until turning golden. Pour in the reserved mussel liquid, increase the heat and bring to the boil, then boil for 2 minutes, or until almost dry. Add the tomato, tomato paste and sugar, then reduce the heat and simmer for 5 minutes. Add the vinegar and simmer for another 5 minutes.

Add the mussels to the saucepan and cook for 1 minute, or until heated through. Spoon into a warm serving dish. Top with the crumbled feta and thyme. Serve hot.

PREPARATION TIME: 45 MINUTES   COOKING TIME: 25 MINUTES

NOTE: Saganaki refers to the utensil used to cook the food in. It is a frying pan with two handles, used for cooking a range of meze, as it can be transferred from stovetop to table. Any pan of a suitable size can be used.

BOREK OF ASPARAGUS

16 asparagus spears
2 tablespoons finely grated lemon zest
2 sheets ready-rolled puff pastry
1 egg yolk
1 tablespoon sesame seeds
tzatziki, to serve (page 153)

MAKES 16

Preheat the oven to 200°C (400°F/Gas 6). Grease two baking trays.

Add the asparagus to a large saucepan of lightly salted boiling water and simmer for 3 minutes. Drain and refresh under cold water. Trim to 10 cm (4 inch) lengths. Combine ½ teaspoon salt, ½ teaspoon pepper and the lemon zest in a shallow dish and roll each asparagus spear in this mixture.

Cut the pastry sheets into sixteen 12 x 6 cm (4½ x 2½ inch) rectangles and put one asparagus spear on each piece of pastry. In a bowl, combine the egg yolk with 2 teaspoons water and brush some on the sides and ends of the pastry. Roll up like a parcel, enclosing the sides so that the asparagus is completely sealed in. Press the joins of the pastry with a fork.

Place the parcels on the prepared trays. Brush with the remaining egg and sprinkle with sesame seeds. Bake for 15–20 minutes, or until golden. Serve warm or cold, with tzatziki

PREPARATION TIME: 20 MINUTES   COOKING TIME: 25 MINUTES

BOREK OF MUSHROOM

1 tablespoon olive oil
1 onion, chopped
¼ teaspoon paprika
4 bacon slices, cut into 5 mm (¼ inch) cubes
250 g (9 oz) mushrooms, cut into 5 mm (¼ inch) cubes
6 sheets ready-rolled puff pastry

MAKES 24

Heat the olive oil in a frying pan over medium heat, add the onion and paprika and cook for 3 minutes, without browning. Add the bacon and cook for 3 minutes, then add the mushroom and cook for 5 minutes, or until all the ingredients are tender. Season with salt and pepper, then spoon into a bowl. Set aside and allow to cool completely.

Using a 10 cm (4 inch) pastry cutter, cut four rounds out of each sheet of pastry. Refrigerate to make handling them easier. Preheat the oven to 200°C (400°F/Gas 6). Grease two baking trays.

Spoon 1 tablespoon of the mushroom mixture into the centre of each round of pastry. Draw up the pastry to form four sides. To seal, pinch the sides together with wet fingertips. Repeat with the remaining pastry and filling. Bake on the prepared trays for 20–30 minutes, or until the pastry is golden brown. Serve hot or warm.

PREPARATION TIME: 40 MINUTES +   COOKING TIME: 40 MINUTES

IMAM BAYILDI

185 ml (6 fl oz/³/4 cup) olive oil
1 kg (2 lb 4 oz) elongated eggplants (aubergines), cut in half lengthways
3 onions, thinly sliced
3 garlic cloves, finely chopped
400 g (14 oz) tinned chopped tomatoes
2 teaspoons dried oregano
4 tablespoons chopped flat-leaf (Italian) parsley
35 g (1¼ oz/¼ cup) currants
¼ teaspoon ground cinnamon
2 tablespoons lemon juice
pinch of sugar
125 ml (4 fl oz/½ cup) tomato juice

SERVES 4–6

Preheat the oven to 180° (350°F/Gas 4). Heat half the olive oil in a large heavy-based frying pan and cook the eggplants on all sides for about 8–10 minutes, until the cut sides are golden. Remove from the pan and scoop out some of the flesh, leaving the skins intact and some flesh lining the skins. Finely chop the scooped-out flesh and set aside.

Heat the remaining olive oil in the same frying pan and cook the onion over medium heat for 8–10 minutes, until transparent. Add the garlic and cook for another minute. Add the tomatoes, oregano, parsley, currants, cinnamon and chopped eggplant flesh and season with salt and pepper.

Place the eggplant shells in a large ovenproof dish and fill each shell with the tomato mixture.

Combine the lemon juice, sugar, tomato juice and some salt and pour a little over each eggplant. Cover with foil and bake for 30 minutes, then uncover and cook for a further 10 minutes. To serve, place the eggplants on a serving platter and lightly drizzle with any remaining juice. Serve with crusty bread.

PREPARATION TIME: 15 MINUTES   COOKING TIME: 1 HOUR

NOTE: This famous Turkish baked eggplant dish is best served at room temperature and makes an excellent first course.

CHILLI GARLIC PRAWNS

1 kg (2 lb 4 oz) raw prawns (shrimp)
60 g (2¼ oz) butter
80 ml (2½ fl oz/⅓ cup) olive oil
3 garlic cloves, roughly chopped
¼ teaspoon chilli flakes
½ teaspoon paprika

SERVES 4–6

Peel the prawns, leaving the tails intact. Gently pull out the dark vein from each prawn back, starting at the head end. Mix the prawns with ½ teaspoon salt in a large bowl, cover and refrigerate for 30 minutes.

Heat the butter and oil in a flameproof dish over medium heat. When foaming, add the garlic and chilli and stir for 1 minute, or until golden. Add the prawns, cook for 3–6 minutes, or until they change colour, then sprinkle with paprika. Serve hot with crusty bread.

PREPARATION TIME: 30 MINUTES +   COOKING TIME: 10 MINUTES

RICE-STUFFED TOMATOES

8 tomatoes
110 g (3¾ oz/½ cup) short-grain rice
2 tablespoons olive oil
1 red onion, finely chopped
1 garlic clove, crushed
1 teaspoon dried oregano
40 g (1½ oz/¼ cup) pine nuts
35 g (1¼ oz/¼ cup) currants
2 handfuls basil, chopped
2 tablespoons chopped flat-leaf (Italian) parsley
1 tablespoon chopped dill
olive oil, for brushing

MAKES 8

Preheat the oven to 160°C (315°F/Gas 2–3). Lightly oil a large ovenproof dish. Slice the top off each tomato and reserve the tops. Spoon out the flesh from the tomatoes, then put the flesh in a strainer to drain the juice, reserving the juice. Remove the flesh from the strainer and finely dice. Put the juice and flesh in separate bowls. Drain the tomato shells upside down on a rack.

Cook the rice in a saucepan of lightly salted rapidly boiling water for 10–12 minutes, or until just tender. Drain and set aside to cool.

Heat the olive oil in a frying pan. Add the onion, garlic and oregano and sauté for 8 minutes, or until the onion is tender. Add the pine nuts and currants and cook for another 5 minutes, stirring frequently. Remove from the heat and stir in the basil, parsley and dill. Season with salt and pepper.

Add the onion mixture and reserved tomato flesh to the rice and mix well. Fill the tomato shells with the rice mixture, piling it up over the top. Spoon 1 tablespoon of the reserved tomato juice on top of each tomato and replace the tomato tops. Lightly brush the tomatoes with olive oil and arrange them in the dish. Bake for 20–30 minutes, or until the tomatoes are cooked through. Serve warm or cold.

PREPARATION TIME: 30 MINUTES   COOKING TIME: 55 MINUTES

GOAT'S CHEESE TARTLETS WITH CAPSICUM

250 g (9 oz/2 cups) plain (all-purpose) flour
125 g (4¹/₂ oz) butter, chopped
1 red capsicum (pepper)
150 g (5¹/₂ oz) firm goat's cheese, grated
250 g (9 oz/1 cup) sour cream or crème fraîche
2 eggs
1 garlic clove, crushed
2 teaspoons finely chopped lemon thyme
30 g (1 oz) butter, extra
1 large red onion, halved and thinly sliced
2 teaspoons soft brown sugar
1 teaspoon balsamic vinegar

MAKES ABOUT 48

Preheat the oven to 190°C (375°F/Gas 5). Lightly grease two 12-hole patty pans or mini muffin tins.

Sift the flour with a pinch of salt into a large bowl. Add the butter and rub into the flour with your fingertips until the mixture resembles fine breadcrumbs. Make a well in the centre and stir in up to 4 tablespoons water to form a firm dough. Gently gather together and lift onto a lightly floured surface. Press into a ball, then flatten into a disc. Wrap in plastic wrap and refrigerate for 30 minutes.

Roll out half the dough on a lightly floured surface to 3 mm (¹/₈ inch) thick and cut out 24 rounds with a 5 cm (2 inch) cutter. Place into the patty pans and refrigerate for 10 minutes.

Cut the capsicum into quarters, then remove the seeds and membrane. Put the capsicum quarters, skin side up, under a hot grill (broiler). Cook until the skin blackens and blisters. Remove from the grill and put in a plastic bag until cool, then peel off the skin. Cut the flesh into thin strips.

Mix together the goat's cheese, sour cream, eggs, garlic and lemon thyme. Season with salt and pepper and set aside.

Melt the extra butter in a frying pan and cook the onion for 5 minutes, or until golden brown. Add the brown sugar and vinegar and cook for another 5 minutes, or until caramelised.

Divide half the cheese mixture evenly into the pastry rounds and top with half the capsicum strips and half the caramelised onion. Bake for 20 minutes, or until golden brown. Repeat with the remaining pastry and fillings. Serve immediately.

PREPARATION TIME: 20 MINUTES +   COOKING TIME: 1 HOUR

ARTICHOKE FRITTATA

30 g (1 oz) butter
2 small leeks, white part only, sliced
1 garlic clove, sliced
6 eggs
100 g (3½ oz) bottled marinated artichoke hearts, sliced
1 teaspoon chopped tarragon
lemon juice, to serve

MAKES 8 WEDGES

Heat the butter in a 20 cm (8 inch) non-stick frying pan (with a heatproof handle), add the leek and garlic and cook until soft. Spread evenly over the bottom of the pan.

Lightly beat the eggs and season with salt and pepper. Pour the eggs into the pan and arrange the artichoke slices on top. Sprinkle with the tarragon and cook over low heat for about 10 minutes, or until set, shaking the pan occasionally to evenly distribute the egg.

Place the pan under a hot grill (broiler) to lightly brown. Cut into wedges and drizzle with a little lemon juice.

PREPARATION TIME: 20 MINUTES   COOKING TIME: 25 MINUTES

MINI TORTILLAS WITH CHORIZO SALSA

4 x 20 cm (8 inch) round flour tortillas
2 tablespoons olive oil
250 g (9 oz) chorizo sausage, cut into small dice
90 g (3¼ oz/⅓ cup) Greek-style yoghurt
1 large handful coriander (cilantro) leaves, finely chopped
1 ripe avocado, cut into small dice
1 large tomato, seeded and cut into small dice
¼ red onion, cut into small dice
2 teaspoons balsamic vinegar
1 tablespoon virgin olive oil
30 small coriander (cilantro) leaves, to garnish

MAKES ABOUT 30

Preheat the oven to 180°C (350°F/Gas 4). Cut seven or eight circles from each tortilla with a 5.5 cm (2¼ inch) cutter, or cut into triangles. Heat 1 tablespoon of the olive oil in a large non-stick frying pan, add one-third of the tortilla circles and cook in a single layer, turning once, until crisp and golden. Drain on crumpled paper towel. Repeat with the remaining oil and tortillas.

Put the chorizo on a baking tray and bake for 10 minutes, or until cooked through. Cool, then drain on crumpled paper towel. Meanwhile, combine the yoghurt and chopped coriander in a small bowl and set aside.

Combine the avocado, tomato and onion in a bowl. Add the chorizo, vinegar and oil and season with salt and pepper. Gently stir to combine.

To assemble, spoon the sausage mixture onto the tortillas and top with the coriander yoghurt. Garnish with the small coriander leaves.

PREPARATION TIME: 25 MINUTES   COOKING TIME: 15 MINUTES

ROLLED SARDINES WITH CUCUMBER

30 butterflied sardines, without heads
(see Note)
2 tablespoons olive oil
2 tablespoons vegetable oil
2 tablespoons lemon juice
2 garlic cloves, sliced
1 tablespoon oregano
1 Lebanese (short) cucumber
1/4 teaspoon sugar
tzatziki, to serve (page 153)

MAKES 30

Put half the sardines in a single layer in a non-metallic dish. Combine the olive oil, vegetable oil, lemon juice, garlic and oregano and pour half over the sardines. Top with the remaining sardines and pour over the rest of the oil mixture. Cover with plastic wrap and marinate in the refrigerator for 30 minutes.

Meanwhile, using a wide vegetable peeler, peel strips lengthways off the cucumber, making four even sides and avoiding peeling off any cucumber with seeds. You should end up with about 15 slices of cucumber. Cut in half to make 30 strips the same length as the sardines.

Lay the cucumber strips flat around the side and base of a colander and sprinkle with the sugar and a little salt. Place the colander over a bowl and leave for 15 minutes to drain off any juices.

Preheat the grill (broiler). Wash the cucumber strips well and pat dry with paper towel. Place one strip of cucumber on the flesh side of each sardine and roll up like a pinwheel. Secure with toothpicks. Place half the sardines under the grill and cook for 5 minutes, or until cooked through. Repeat with the remaining sardines. Serve warm, with tzatziki.

PREPARATION TIME: 20 MINUTES +   COOKING TIME: 10 MINUTES

NOTE: Butterflied sardines are sardines that have been gutted, deboned and opened out flat. The sardines can be rolled in the cucumber a day ahead. Keep covered in the refrigerator.

BROAD BEANS WITH HAM

20 g ($^3/_4$ oz) butter
1 onion, chopped
180 g (6$^1/_2$ oz) serrano ham, roughly chopped (see Note)
2 garlic cloves, crushed
500 g (1 lb 2 oz) broad (fava) beans, fresh or frozen
125 ml (4 fl oz/$^1/_2$ cup) dry white wine
185 ml (6 fl oz/$^3/_4$ cup) chicken stock

SERVES 4

Melt the butter in a large saucepan and add the onion, ham and garlic. Cook over medium heat for 5 minutes, stirring often, until the onion softens.

Add the broad beans and wine and cook over high heat until reduced by half. Add the stock, reduce the heat, then cover and cook for 10 minutes. Uncover and simmer for another 10 minutes. Serve hot as a vegetable accompaniment to meat, or warm as a snack with crusty bread.

PREPARATION TIME: 10 MINUTES   COOKING TIME: 30 MINUTES

NOTE: Instead of serrano ham, you can use thickly sliced prosciutto.

PICKLED SQUID

1 kg (2 lb 4 oz) small squid
4 fresh bay leaves
4 oregano sprigs
10 whole black peppercorns
2 teaspoons coriander seeds
1 small red chilli, halved and seeded
625 ml (21$^1/_2$ fl oz/2$^1/_2$ cups) white wine vinegar
2–3 tablespoons olive oil
lemon wedges, to serve
chopped flat-leaf (Italian) parsley, to serve

SERVES 4

To prepare the squid, grasp each squid body in one hand and the head and tentacles in the other and pull apart to separate them. Cut the tentacles from the head by cutting below the eyes. Discard the head. Push out the beak and discard. Pull the quill from inside the body and discard. Under cold running water, pull away the skin (the flaps can be used). Cut into 8 mm ($^3/_8$ inch) rings.

Put 2 litres (70 fl oz/8 cups) water and 1 bay leaf in a large saucepan. Bring to the boil and add the squid rings and 1 teaspoon salt. Reduce the heat and simmer for 5 minutes. Drain and dry well.

Pack the squid rings into a sterilised, dry 500 ml (17 fl oz/2 cup) jar with a sealing lid (see Note, page 149). Add the oregano, peppercorns, coriander seeds, chilli and remaining bay leaves. Cover completely with the vinegar, then gently pour in enough olive oil to cover by 2 cm ($^3/_4$ inch). Seal and refrigerate for 1 week before opening. When you are ready to serve, remove from the marinade, place on a serving dish and garnish with lemon wedges and chopped parsley.

PREPARATION TIME: 30 MINUTES +   COOKING TIME: 5 MINUTES

CHICKPEAS WITH CHORIZO SAUSAGE

165 g (5³/4 oz/³/4 cup) dried chickpeas
1 bay leaf
4 cloves
1 cinnamon stick
1 litre (35 fl oz/4 cups) chicken stock
2 tablespoons olive oil
1 onion, finely chopped
1 garlic clove, crushed
pinch dried thyme
375 g (13 oz) chorizo sausages, chopped
1 tablespoon chopped flat-leaf (Italian) parsley

SERVES 6

Put the chickpeas in a large bowl, cover well with water and soak overnight. Drain, then put in a large saucepan with the bay leaf, cloves, cinnamon stick and stock. Top up with a little water so the chickpeas are well covered in liquid, bring to the boil, then reduce the heat and simmer for 1 hour, or until the chickpeas are tender. If they need more time, add a little more water. There should be just a little liquid left in the saucepan. Drain and remove the bay leaf, cloves and cinnamon stick.

Heat the olive oil in a large frying pan, add the onion and cook over medium heat for 3 minutes, or until translucent. Add the garlic and thyme and cook, stirring, for 1 minute. Increase the heat to medium–high, add the chorizo and cook for a further 3 minutes.

Add the chickpeas to the frying pan, mix well, then stir over medium heat until they are heated through. Remove from the heat and stir in the parsley. Taste before seasoning with salt and freshly ground black pepper. This dish is equally delicious served hot or at room temperature.

PREPARATION TIME: 15 MINUTES +   COOKING TIME: 1 HOUR 10 MINUTES

DESSERTS

ALMOND MASCARPONE CREPES WITH SUMMER FRUIT

ALMOND MASCARPONE
60 g (2¼ oz/½ cup) slivered almonds
115 g (4 oz/½ cup) caster (superfine) sugar
500 g (1 lb 2 oz) mascarpone cheese

250 g (9 oz) strawberries, sliced
1 tablespoon caster (superfine) sugar
125 g (4½ oz/1 cup) plain (all-purpose) flour
2 eggs
125 ml (4 fl oz/½ cup) milk
30 g (1 oz) unsalted butter, melted
melted butter, extra, to grease
4 kiwi fruit, thinly sliced
200 g (7 oz) raspberries
250 g (9 oz) blueberries

MAKES ABOUT 12 CREPES

To make the almond mascarpone, preheat the grill (broiler) to low and grill (broil) the almonds until lightly golden, then place on a greased baking tray. Put the sugar in a small heavy-based saucepan with 125 ml (4 fl oz/½ cup) water and stir, without boiling, until the sugar has dissolved. Bring to the boil, then reduce the heat and simmer, without stirring, for 15 minutes, or until the liquid turns golden brown. Quickly pour over the almonds and leave to set. Break into chunks and finely grind in a food processor, transfer to a bowl, then stir in the mascarpone, cover and refrigerate.

Place the strawberries in a large bowl and sprinkle with the sugar. Stir to combine, then refrigerate.

Combine the flour, eggs and milk in a food processor for 10 seconds. Add 125 ml (4 fl oz/½ cup) water and the melted butter and process until smooth. Pour into a jug and set aside for 30 minutes.

Heat a small crepe pan or non-stick frying pan and brush lightly with the extra melted butter. Pour 60 ml (2 fl oz/¼ cup) batter into the pan, swirling to cover the base thinly. Cook for about 30 seconds, or until the edges just begin to curl, then turn the crepe over and cook the other side until lightly browned. Transfer to a plate and cover with a tea towel while cooking the remaining batter.

Spread each warm crepe with almond mascarpone and fold into quarters. Serve the crepes topped with the strawberries, kiwi fruit, raspberries and blueberries.

PREPARATION TIME: 40 MINUTES +   COOKING TIME: 35 MINUTES

NOTE: The crepes can be made ahead of time. Place a piece of baking paper between each crepe, wrap in foil, then plastic and refrigerate or freeze.

CHOCOLATE BAVAROIS

200 g (7 oz/1⅓ cups) chopped dark chocolate
375 ml (13 fl oz/1½ cups) milk
4 egg yolks
80 g (2¾ oz/⅓ cup) caster (superfine) sugar
1 tablespoon gelatine powder
310 ml (10¾ fl oz/1¼ cups) whipping cream

SERVES 6

Combine the chocolate and milk in a small saucepan. Stir over low heat until the chocolate has melted and the milk just comes to the boil. Remove from the heat.

Beat the egg yolks and sugar until combined, then gradually add the hot chocolate milk, whisking until combined. Return to a clean saucepan and cook over low heat until the mixture thickens enough to coat the back of a wooden spoon. Do not allow it to boil. Remove from the heat.

Put 2 tablespoons water in a small heatproof bowl, sprinkle the gelatine in an even layer over the surface and leave to go spongy. Stir into the hot chocolate mixture until dissolved. Refrigerate until the mixture is cold but not set, stirring occasionally.

Beat the cream until soft peaks form, then fold into the chocolate mixture in two batches. Pour into six 250 ml (9 fl oz/1 cup) glasses and refrigerate for several hours or overnight, or until set.

PREPARATION TIME: 30 MINUTES +   COOKING TIME: 10 MINUTES

CHOCOLATE RUM MOUSSE

250 g (9 oz/1⅔ cups) chopped dark chocolate
3 eggs
55 g (2 oz/¼ cup) caster (superfine) sugar
250 ml (9 fl oz/1 cup) whipping cream
2 teaspoons dark rum

SERVES 4

Put the chocolate in a heatproof bowl. Half-fill a saucepan with water and bring to the boil, then remove the pan from the heat. Sit the bowl over the pan, making sure the base of the bowl doesn't touch the water. Stir occasionally until the chocolate has melted. Set aside to cool.

Using electric beaters, beat the eggs and caster sugar in a small bowl for 5 minutes, or until thick, pale and increased in volume. Transfer the mixture to a large bowl. In another small bowl, lightly whip the cream.

Using a metal spoon, fold the melted chocolate and the rum into the beaten eggs, leave the mixture to cool, then fold in the whipped cream until just combined. Spoon into four 250 ml (9 fl oz/1 cup) ramekins or dessert glasses. Refrigerate for 2 hours, or until set.

PREPARATION TIME: 20 MINUTES +   COOKING TIME: 5 MINUTES

Chocolate bavarois

HAZELNUT TORTE

6 egg whites
280 g (10 oz/1$\frac{1}{4}$ cups) caster (superfine) sugar
180 g (6$\frac{1}{2}$ oz) ground hazelnuts
2 tablespoons plain (all-purpose) flour, sifted
100 ml (3$\frac{1}{2}$ fl oz) white rum
chopped roasted hazelnuts, to decorate

CHOCOLATE LEAVES
150 g (5$\frac{1}{2}$ oz) white chocolate, chopped
non-toxic leaves (choose leaves with prominent veins)

WHITE CHOCOLATE CREAM
125 g (4$\frac{1}{2}$ oz) white chocolate, chopped
435 ml (15$\frac{1}{4}$ fl oz/1$\frac{3}{4}$ cups) whipping cream

DARK CHOCOLATE CREAM
40 g (1$\frac{1}{2}$ oz) dark chocolate
125 ml (4 fl oz/$\frac{1}{2}$ cup) whipping cream

SERVES 8–10

Lightly grease two 20 cm (8 inch) cake tins. Line the bases with baking paper and then grease the paper. Dust the tins lightly with flour, shaking off any excess. Preheat the oven to 180°C (350°F/Gas 4).

Beat the egg whites in a clean, dry bowl with electric beaters until stiff peaks form. Gradually add the sugar, beating until thick and glossy. Lightly fold in the ground hazelnuts and flour. Divide the mixture evenly between the prepared tins and smooth the tops with wet fingers. Bake for 15–20 minutes, or until the cakes feel spongy to touch. Leave in the tins to cool a little before turning out onto wire racks to cool completely. Cut each cake in half horizontally with a long serrated knife.

To make the chocolate leaves, put the white chocolate in a heatproof bowl. Half-fill a saucepan with water and bring to the boil, then remove the pan from the heat. Sit the bowl over the pan, making sure the base of the bowl doesn't touch the water. Stir occasionally until the chocolate has melted. Use a fine brush to paint the chocolate over the underside of the leaves. Leave to set, then peel away the leaf. If the coating of chocolate is too thin, it will break when the leaf is removed.

To make the white chocolate cream, put the chocolate in a heatproof bowl. Half-fill a saucepan with water and bring to the boil, then remove the pan from the heat. Sit the bowl over the pan, making sure the base of the bowl doesn't touch the water. Stir occasionally until the chocolate melts, then allow to cool. Whip the cream in a bowl with electric beaters until it begins to hold its shape. Add the chocolate and beat it in, then allow to cool. Make the dark chocolate cream in the same way.

Put a layer of cake on a serving plate, brush the cut surface with a little rum and spread with a quarter of the white chocolate cream. Top with a second cake layer. Brush with rum and spread with all the dark chocolate cream. Add another layer of cake and spread with rum and a quarter of the white chocolate cream. Top with the final cake layer and spread the remaining white chocolate cream over the top and side of the cake. Decorate the torte with the chopped hazelnuts and chocolate leaves.

PREPARATION TIME: 1 HOUR   COOKING TIME: 35 MINUTES

CHILLED LIME SOUFFLÉ

caster (superfine) sugar, to coat
melted butter
5 eggs, separated
230 g (8 oz/1 cup) caster (superfine) sugar
2 teaspoons finely grated lime zest
185 ml (6 fl oz/^{3}/$_4$ cup) lime juice, strained
1 tablespoon gelatine powder
310 ml (10^3/$_4$ fl oz/1^1/$_4$ cups) whipping cream

SERVES 4

Cut four strips of baking paper or foil long enough to fit around 250 ml (9 fl oz/1 cup) soufflé dishes or ramekins. Fold each in half lengthways, wrap one around each dish, extending 4 cm (1^1/$_2$ inches) above the rim, then secure with string. Brush the inside of the collar with melted butter, sprinkle with caster sugar, shake to coat, then tip out the excess.

Using electric beaters, beat the egg yolks, sugar and lime zest in a small bowl for 3 minutes, or until the sugar has dissolved and the mixture is thick and pale. Heat the lime juice in a small saucepan, then gradually add the lime juice to the yolk mixture while beating, until well mixed.

Pour 60 ml (2 fl oz/^{1}/$_4$ cup) water into a small heatproof bowl, sprinkle the gelatine in an even layer over the surface and leave to go spongy. Bring a large saucepan filled with 4 cm (1^1/$_2$ inches) water to the boil, remove from the heat and carefully lower the gelatine bowl into the water (it should come halfway up the side of the bowl). Stir until dissolved. Cool slightly, then add gradually to the lime mixture, beating on low speed until combined. Transfer to a large bowl, cover with plastic wrap and refrigerate for 15 minutes, or until thickened but not set.

In a small bowl, lightly whip the cream. Using a metal spoon, fold the cream into the lime mixture until almost combined.

Using electric beaters, beat the egg whites in a clean, dry bowl until soft peaks form. Fold the egg white quickly and lightly into the lime mixture, using a large metal spoon, until just combined with no lumps of egg white remaining. Spoon gently into the soufflé dishes and chill until set. Just before serving, remove the collars and serve topped with grated lime zest or whipped cream if desired.

PREPARATION TIME: 35 MINUTES +   COOKING TIME: 5 MINUTES

BAKED LIME AND PASSIONFRUIT CHEESECAKE

250 g (9 oz) plain sweet biscuits
125 g (4$\frac{1}{2}$ oz) unsalted butter, melted

FILLING
500 g (1 lb 2 oz) cream cheese, softened
to room temperature
80 g (2$\frac{3}{4}$ oz/$\frac{1}{3}$ cup) caster (superfine)
sugar
3 teaspoons finely grated lime zest
2 tablespoons lime juice
2 eggs, lightly beaten
125 g (4$\frac{1}{2}$ oz/$\frac{1}{2}$ cup) passionfruit pulp
(see Note)

PASSIONFRUIT TOPPING
1 tablespoon caster (superfine) sugar
3 teaspoons cornflour (cornstarch)
125 g (4$\frac{1}{2}$ oz/$\frac{1}{2}$ cup) passionfruit pulp

SERVES 6–8

Lightly grease a 20 cm (8 inch) diameter spring-form cake tin and line the base with baking paper. Preheat the oven to 160°C (315°F/Gas 2–3). Finely crush the biscuits in a food processor and mix in the butter. Spoon into the tin and press firmly into the base and side of the tin. Chill for 30 minutes.

Using electric beaters, beat the cream cheese, sugar, lime zest and lime juice until creamy. Gradually beat in the eggs and passionfruit pulp. Pour into the tin, put on a baking tray to catch any drips, and bake for 45–50 minutes, or until just set. Cool completely.

To make the passionfruit topping, combine the sugar, cornflour and 2 tablespoons water in a small saucepan over low heat. Stir until smooth, then add 2 more tablespoons water and the passionfruit pulp and stir until the mixture boils and thickens. Pour the hot topping over the cooled cheesecake, spread evenly and cool completely. Refrigerate overnight. Serve with whipped cream if desired.

PREPARATION TIME: 50 MINUTES +   COOKING TIME: 55 MINUTES

NOTE: You will need to use the pulp from about eight fresh passionfruit for this recipe.

WHITE CHOCOLATE FONDUE WITH FRUIT

125 ml (4 fl oz/^{1}/$_2$ cup) light corn syrup
170 ml (5^1/$_2$ fl oz/^{2}/$_3$ cup) thick (double/heavy) cream
60 ml (2 fl oz/^{1}/$_4$ cup) Cointreau or orange-flavoured liqueur
250 g (9 oz) white chocolate, chopped marshmallows and fresh fruit such as sliced peaches, strawberries and cherries

SERVES 6–8

Combine the corn syrup and cream in a small pan or fondue. Bring to the boil, then remove from the heat.

Add the liqueur and white chocolate and stir until melted. Serve with marshmallows and fresh fruit.

PREPARATION TIME: 15 MINUTES   COOKING TIME: 10 MINUTES

MANGO FOOL

3 large mangoes
250 ml (9 fl oz/1 cup) custard
420 ml (14^1/$_2$ fl oz/1^2/$_3$ cups) whipping cream

SERVES 6

Peel and stone the mangoes and purée the flesh in a food processor. Add the custard and blend to combine.

Whip the cream until soft peaks form, then gently fold into the mango mixture until just combined — do not overmix, as you want to end up with a decorative marbled effect.

Pour the mixture into a serving dish or individual glasses. Gently smooth the top, then refrigerate for at least 1 hour before serving. Serve with fresh fruit if desired.

PREPARATION TIME: 20 MINUTES +   COOKING TIME: NIL

White chocolate fondue with fruit

PAVLOVA WITH FRESH FRUIT

4 egg whites
230 g (8 oz/1 cup) caster (superfine) sugar
375 ml (13 fl oz/1½ cups) cream, whipped
1 banana, sliced
125 g (4½ oz) raspberries
125 g (4½ oz) blueberries

SERVES 8

Preheat the oven to 150°C (300°F/Gas 2). Line a baking tray with baking paper. Mark a 20 cm (8 inch) circle on the paper as a guide for the pavlova base if you find it easier.

Put the egg whites in a large, very clean, dry stainless steel or glass bowl — any hint of grease will prevent the egg whites foaming. Leave the whites for a few minutes to reach room temperature, then, using electric beaters, beat slowly until the whites start to become a frothy foam, then increase the speed until the bubbles in the foam have become small and even-sized. When the foam forms stiff peaks, add the sugar gradually, beating constantly after each addition, until the mixture is thick and glossy and all the sugar has dissolved. Don't overbeat or the mixture will become grainy.

Spread the mixture on the paper and shape it evenly into a circle, running a flat-bladed knife or spatula around the edge and over the top. Run the knife up the edge of the mixture, all the way around, to make furrows. This will strengthen the pavlova and give it a decorative finish.

Bake for 40 minutes, or until pale and crisp, then turn off the oven and cool the pavlova in the oven with the door ajar. When cold, decorate with whipped cream, banana, raspberries and blueberries.

PREPARATION TIME: 20 MINUTES   COOKING TIME: 40 MINUTES

NOTE: The meringue can be cooked in advance and kept overnight in an airtight container. Serve within 1 hour of decorating.

STUFFED FIGS

175 g (6 oz/¹/₂ cup) honey
125 ml (4 fl oz/¹/₂ cup) sweet dark sherry
¹/₄ teaspoon ground cinnamon
18 large dried figs
18 whole blanched almonds
100 g (3¹/₂ oz) dark chocolate,
cut into shards
thick (double/heavy) cream, to serve

MAKES 18

Put the honey, sherry, cinnamon, figs and 375 ml (13 fl oz/1¹/₂ cups) water in a large saucepan over high heat. Bring to the boil, then reduce the heat and simmer for 10 minutes. Remove the pan from the heat and set aside for 3 hours. Remove the figs with a slotted spoon, reserving the liquid. Preheat the oven to 180°C (350°F/Gas 4).

Return the pan of liquid to the stovetop and boil over high heat for 5 minutes, or until syrupy, then set aside.

Cut the stems from the figs, then cut a slit in the top of each fig. Push an almond and a few shards of chocolate into each slit. Put the figs in a lightly buttered ovenproof dish and bake for 15 minutes, or until the chocolate has melted. Serve with a little of the syrup and some cream.

PREPARATION TIME: 30 MINUTES +   COOKING TIME: 30 MINUTES

RHUBARB AND PEAR CRUMBLE

600 g (1 lb 5 oz) rhubarb
2 strips lemon zest
1 tablespoon honey, or to taste
2 firm ripe pears
50 g (1³/₄ oz/¹/₂ cup) rolled (porridge) oats
50 g (1³/₄ oz/¹/₃ cup) wholemeal
plain (all-purpose) flour
60 g (2¹/₄ oz/¹/₃ cup) soft brown sugar
50 g (1³/₄ oz) unsalted butter

SERVES 6

Trim the rhubarb, then wash it and cut into 3 cm (1¹/₄ inch) pieces. Put the rhubarb in a saucepan with the lemon zest and 1 tablespoon water. Cook, covered, over low heat for 10 minutes, or until tender. Cool a little, then stir in the honey. Remove the lemon zest and discard.

Preheat the oven to 180°C (350°F/Gas 4). Peel and core the pears, then cut them into 2 cm (³/₄ inch) cubes and combine with the rhubarb. Pour into a 1.25 litre (44 fl oz/5 cup) ovenproof dish and smooth the surface.

To make the crumble topping, combine the rolled oats, wholemeal flour and brown sugar in a bowl. Rub in the butter using your fingertips, until the mixture looks crumbly. Spread the crumble evenly over the fruit. Bake for about 15 minutes, or until cooked and golden. Serve with whipped cream or ice cream.

PREPARATION TIME: 20 MINUTES   COOKING TIME: 25 MINUTES

CHARLOTTE MALAKOFF

250 g (9 oz) savoiardi (lady finger) biscuits
125 ml (4 fl oz/¹/₂ cup) Grand Marnier
500 g (1 lb 2 oz) strawberries, hulled and halved
whipped cream and strawberries, to serve

ALMOND CREAM
125 g (4¹/₂ oz) unsalted butter
80 g (2³/₄ oz/¹/₃ cup) caster (superfine) sugar
60 ml (2 fl oz/¹/₄ cup) Grand Marnier
¹/₄ teaspoon almond essence
185 ml (6 fl oz/³/₄ cup) cream, whipped
140 g (5 oz/1¹/₃ cups) ground almonds

SERVES 8–12

Brush a deep 1–1.5 litre (35–52 fl oz/4–6 cup) soufflé dish with melted butter or oil. Line the base with baking paper and grease the paper. Trim the biscuits to fit the height of the dish.

Combine the liqueur with 125 ml (4 fl oz/¹/₂ cup) water. Quickly dip the biscuits into the liqueur mixture and arrange upright around the side of the dish, rounded side down.

To make the almond cream, using electric beaters, beat the butter and sugar until light and creamy. Add the liqueur and almond essence. Continue beating until the mixture is smooth and the sugar has dissolved. Using a metal spoon, fold in the whipped cream and ground almonds.

Place the strawberry halves, cut side down, into the base of the dish. Spoon one-third of the almond cream over the strawberries. Top with a layer of dipped biscuits. Continue layering, finishing with a layer of biscuits, then press down.

Cover with foil and place a small plate and weight on top. Refrigerate for 8 hours, or overnight. Remove the plate and foil and turn onto a chilled serving plate. Remove the baking paper. Decorate with whipped cream and strawberries.

PREPARATION TIME: 1 HOUR +   COOKING TIME: NIL

PEARS POACHED IN GRAPE JUICE

6 beurre bosc (or any very firm) pears
2 tablespoons lemon juice
500 ml (17 fl oz/2 cups) dark grape juice
500 ml (17 fl oz/2 cups) blackcurrant juice
2 tablespoons sweet sherry
4 cloves
1 kg (2 lb 4 oz) black grapes
250 g (9 oz/1 cup) plain yoghurt
1/2 teaspoon ground cinnamon
1 tablespoon honey

SERVES 6

Core and peel the pears, leaving the stalks on. Place the pears, as you peel them, in a bowl filled with cold water and the lemon juice, to prevent them browning.

Put the grape and blackcurrant juices, sherry and cloves in a saucepan large enough to hold the pears. Add the pears. Bring the liquid to the boil, then reduce to a simmer. Cover and cook for 35–40 minutes, or until the pears are tender. Remove the pan from the heat and leave the pears to cool in the syrup. Gently transfer the pears and syrup to a bowl and cover with plastic wrap. Refrigerate overnight.

Strain the syrup into a saucepan, bring to the boil, then reduce the heat and simmer for 40 minutes, or until reduced by about two-thirds.

To serve, arrange the pears and grapes on a large platter. Cool the syrup slightly and pour over the pears. Before serving, thoroughly mix together the yoghurt, cinnamon and honey and spoon over the pears.

PREPARATION TIME: 15 MINUTES +   COOKING TIME: 1 HOUR 20 MINUTES

FIGS POACHED IN RED WINE AND THYME

375 g (13 oz) dried whole figs
250 ml (9 fl oz/1 cup) red wine
235 g (8 1/2 oz/2/3 cup) honey
4 thyme sprigs, tied with string
whipped cream, to serve

SERVES 4

Put the figs in a heatproof bowl, cover with boiling water and leave to soak for 10 minutes, then drain.

Put the wine and honey in a saucepan and warm slightly over low heat. Add the figs and thyme. Cover and simmer for 10 minutes, then uncover and cook for another 10 minutes. Transfer the figs to a bowl and discard the thyme. Bring the syrup to the boil, then boil rapidly for 5–8 minutes, until the syrup has reduced and just coats the back of a spoon.

Return the figs to the saucepan, stir to warm through, then allow to cool slightly. Serve warm or at room temperature with whipped cream.

PREPARATION TIME: 20 MINUTES   COOKING TIME: 30 MINUTES

Pears poached in grape juice

SACHER SQUARES

BASE

125 g (4¹/2 oz/1 cup) plain (all-purpose) flour
60 g (2¹/4 oz) unsalted butter, chopped
60 g (2¹/4 oz/¹/4 cup) sugar
2 egg yolks, lightly beaten

CAKE

125 g (4¹/2 oz/1 cup) plain (all-purpose) flour
40 g (1¹/2 oz/¹/3 cup) unsweetened cocoa powder
230 g (8 oz/1 cup) caster (superfine) sugar
100 g (3¹/2 oz) unsalted butter
2 tablespoons apricot jam
4 eggs, separated
315 g (11 oz/1 cup) apricot jam, extra

TOPPING

250 g (9 oz/1²/3 cups) chopped dark chocolate
185 ml (6 fl oz/³/4 cup) pouring cream

MAKES 24

Preheat the oven to 180°C (350°F/Gas 4). Line a baking tray with baking paper. Lightly grease a shallow 18 x 28 cm (7 x 11¹/4 inch) cake tin and line the base and sides with baking paper, extending over two sides.

To make the base, sift the flour into a large bowl and add the butter. Rub in until the mixture resembles fine breadcrumbs. Stir in the sugar and make a well in the centre. Add the egg yolks and 1¹/2 teaspoons iced water and mix with a flat-bladed knife, using a cutting action, to form a firm dough, adding more water if necessary. Gently gather the dough together and lift onto a lightly floured surface. Roll out the pastry to an 18 x 28 cm (7 x 11¹/4 inch) rectangle. Bake on the prepared tray for 10 minutes, or until just golden. Cool completely.

To make the cake, sift the flour and cocoa into a large bowl. Make a well in the centre. Combine the sugar, butter and jam in a small saucepan and stir over low heat until the butter has melted and the sugar has dissolved. Remove from the heat. Add the butter mixture to the dry ingredients and stir until just combined. Mix in the egg yolks.

Beat the egg whites in a small bowl until soft peaks form. Using a metal spoon, fold the egg whites into the cake mixture. Pour into the prepared tin and bake for 30 minutes, or until a skewer comes out clean when inserted into the centre of the cake. Leave in the tin for 15 minutes before turning out onto a wire rack to cool.

Warm the extra jam in a microwave or in a small pan, then push through a fine sieve. Brush the pastry base with 3 tablespoons of the jam. Place the cake on the base. Trim the sides evenly, cutting the hard edges from the cake and base. Using a serrated knife, cut into 24 squares. Brush the top and sides of each square with jam. Place the squares on a large wire rack, over a piece of baking paper, spacing them 4 cm (1¹/2 inches) apart.

To make the topping, put the chocolate in a small bowl. Put the cream in a small pan and bring to the boil. Remove from the heat, pour the cream over the chocolate and leave for 5 minutes, then stir until the mixture is smooth. Cool slightly. Working with one at a time, spoon the topping over each cake square and use a flat-bladed knife to cover completely. Scrape the excess topping from the paper, with any left-over topping, and spoon into a small piping (icing) bag and pipe an 'S' onto each square.

PREPARATION TIME: 1 HOUR   COOKING TIME: 40 MINUTES

PRALINE ICE CREAM WITH CARAMEL BARK

70 g (2¹/₂ oz) blanched almonds, toasted
55 g (2 oz/¹/₄ cup) caster (superfine) sugar
125 g (4¹/₂ oz) white chocolate, chopped
185 ml (6 fl oz/³/₄ cup) whipping cream
250 g (9 oz) mascarpone cheese
2 tablespoons sugar

SERVES 4

To make the praline, line a baking tray with foil, brush the foil lightly with oil and put the almonds on the foil.

Put the caster sugar in a small saucepan over low heat. Tilt the saucepan slightly, but do not stir, and watch until the sugar melts and turns golden — this should take 3–5 minutes. Pour the caramel over the almonds and leave until set and cold. Break into chunks, put in a plastic bag and crush with a rolling pin, or process briefly in a food processor until crumbly.

Put the white chocolate in a heatproof bowl. Half-fill a saucepan with water and bring to the boil, then remove the pan from the heat. Sit the bowl over the pan, making sure the base of the bowl doesn't touch the water. Stir occasionally until the chocolate has melted. Set aside to cool.

Whip the cream until stiff peaks form. Stir the mascarpone and melted chocolate in a large bowl to combine. Using a metal spoon, fold in the cream and crushed praline. Transfer to a 1 litre (35 fl oz/4 cup) metal tin, cover the surface with baking paper and freeze for 6 hours, or overnight. Remove from the freezer 15 minutes before serving, to soften slightly.

To make the caramel bark, line a baking tray with foil and brush lightly with oil. Sprinkle the sugar evenly onto the tray and place under a hot grill (broiler) for 2 minutes, until the sugar has melted and is golden. Check frequently towards the end of cooking time, as the sugar may burn quickly. Remove from the heat, leave until set and completely cold, then break into shards. Serve with the ice cream.

PREPARATION TIME: 25 MINUTES +   COOKING TIME: 10 MINUTES

CHOCOLATE CHERRY TRIFLE

350 g (12 oz) ready-made chocolate cake
900 g (2 lb) tinned pitted dark cherries
60 ml (2 fl oz/¼ cup) kirsch or
cherry liqueur
185 ml (6 fl oz/¾ cup) whipping cream
2 egg yolks
2 tablespoons sugar
1 tablespoon cornflour (cornstarch)
250 ml (9 fl oz/1 cup) milk
1 teaspoon natural vanilla extract
30 g (1 oz/¼ cup) slivered almonds,
toasted
whipped cream, extra, to serve

SERVES 6

Cut the cake into thin strips. Line the base of a 1.75 litre (61 fl oz/7 cup) serving bowl with one-third of the cake.

Drain the cherries, reserving the juice. Combine 250 ml (9 fl oz/1 cup) of the juice with the liqueur and sprinkle some liberally over the cake. Spoon some cherries over the cake.

To make the custard, lightly whip the cream and set it aside. Whisk the egg yolks, sugar and cornflour in a heatproof bowl until thick and pale. Heat the milk in a saucepan until almost boiling. Remove from the heat and add gradually to the egg mixture, beating constantly. Return to a clean saucepan and stir over medium heat for 5 minutes, or until the custard boils and thickens. Remove from the heat and add the vanilla. Cover the surface with plastic wrap and allow to cool, then fold in the whipped cream.

To assemble, spoon a third of the custard over the cherries and cake in the bowl. Top with more cake, syrup, cherries and custard. Repeat the layering process, ending with custard on top. Cover and refrigerate for 3–4 hours. Decorate with almonds and whipped cream.

PREPARATION TIME: 30 MINUTES +   COOKING TIME: 10 MINUTES

PEACHES AND CREAM TRIFLE

1 day-old sponge cake, cut into cubes
825 g (1 lb 13 oz) tinned sliced peaches
60 ml (2 fl oz/¼ cup) sweet Marsala,
peach schnapps liqueur
or Grand Marnier
250 ml (9 fl oz/1 cup) whipping cream
200 g (7 oz) mascarpone cheese
25 g (1 oz/¼ cup) flaked almonds,
toasted

SERVES 6–8

Put the cake cubes in a 2 litre (70 fl oz/8 cup) dish and press down firmly. Drain the peaches, reserving 125 ml (4 fl oz/½ cup) of the juice. Mix the Marsala with the juice and drizzle over the cake.

Arrange the peach slices over the cake. Beat the cream until soft peaks form, then add the mascarpone and beat briefly, to just mix. Spread the cream mixture over the peaches. Refrigerate for 1 hour to allow the flavours to develop. Sprinkle with almonds just before serving.

PREPARATION TIME: 20 MINUTES +   COOKING TIME: NIL

CHOCOLATE PUDDING

125 g (4½ oz) dark chocolate, chopped
90 g (3¼ oz) unsalted butter, at room temperature
95 g (3¼ oz/½ cup) soft brown sugar
3 eggs, separated
1 teaspoon natural vanilla extract
125 g (4½ oz/1 cup) self-raising flour
1 tablespoon unsweetened cocoa powder
½ teaspoon bicarbonate of soda (baking soda)
60 ml (2 fl oz/¼ cup) milk
2 tablespoons brandy
whipped cream, to serve

CHOCOLATE SAUCE
125 g (4½ oz) dark chocolate, chopped
60 ml (2 fl oz/¼ cup) pouring cream
1 tablespoon brandy

SERVES 6

Grease a 1.25 litre (44 fl oz/5 cup) pudding basin and line the base with a circle of baking paper. Preheat the oven to 180°C (350°F/Gas 4).

Put the chocolate in a heatproof bowl. Half-fill a saucepan with water and bring to the boil, then remove the pan from the heat. Sit the bowl over the pan, making sure the base of the bowl doesn't touch the water. Stir occasionally until the chocolate has melted. Set aside to cool. Keep the saucepan of water for later, for making the chocolate sauce.

Cream the butter and half the brown sugar until light and creamy. Beat in the egg yolks, melted chocolate and vanilla. Sift together the flour, cocoa and bicarbonate of soda. Fold into the mixture, alternating with spoonfuls of the combined milk and brandy.

Beat the egg whites in a clean, dry bowl until soft peaks form. Gradually beat in the remaining sugar, until stiff and glossy, then fold into the chocolate mixture.

Pour into the prepared basin. Cover tightly with foil and secure with string. Put in a deep ovenproof dish and pour in enough hot water to come halfway up the side of the basin. Bake for 1¼ hours, or until a skewer comes out clean. Unmould onto a serving plate.

To make the chocolate sauce, put the chocolate, cream and brandy in a heatproof bowl. Reheat the saucepan of water, bring to the boil, then remove the pan from the heat. Sit the bowl over the pan, making sure the base of the bowl doesn't touch the water. Stir occasionally until the chocolate has melted and the sauce is smooth. Serve the pudding with the chocolate sauce and with whipped cream.

PREPARATION TIME: 20 MINUTES   COOKING TIME: 1 HOUR 25 MINUTES

SORBET BALLS

400 g (14 oz) sorbet
250 g (9 oz/1²/₃ cups) dark chocolate melts (buttons)

MAKES 24

Soften the sorbet slightly and spread it out in a shallow container to a depth of about 2.5 cm (1 inch). Put in the freezer until solid.

Cover a baking tray with baking paper and place in the freezer. Using a melon baller, scoop out tiny balls of sorbet and place them on the prepared tray. Put a cocktail stick in each sorbet ball. Cover the tray tightly with plastic wrap, ensuring it is completely covered so the sorbet doesn't dry out, then refreeze overnight so the balls are solid.

Place the chocolate in a heatproof bowl. Bring a saucepan of water to the boil, then remove the pan from the heat. Sit the bowl over the pan, making sure the base of the bowl doesn't touch the water. Stir occasionally until the chocolate has melted. Remove the bowl and set aside to cool a little.

Ladle some of the melted chocolate into a separate bowl so that if anything goes wrong you won't ruin the whole batch. Work with just a few balls at a time so they do not melt. Dip each sorbet ball in the chocolate, making sure it is thoroughly coated and place it back on the tray. Return to the freezer. Reheat the chocolate if necessary. It must be liquid enough not to coat too thickly. Add more melted chocolate to the bowl when necessary, but if it seizes, start with a new bowl and a new batch. Freeze until you are ready to serve. Serve these on a bed of crushed ice or pile them into an iced bowl (see Note).

PREPARATION TIME: 20 MINUTES +   COOKING TIME: 5 MINUTES

NOTE: To make an ice bowl, fill a bowl half-full of water and float some flower petals and herb leaves in it, place another bowl inside and weigh it down so it sits down in the water but does not sink to the bottom. The water should form a bowl-shaped layer between the two bowls. Freeze overnight. Separate the bowls by rubbing a cloth dipped in hot water over them and twisting them apart.

SWEET COUSCOUS

80 g (2³/4 oz) combined pistachio nuts,
pine nuts and blanched almonds
45 g (1¹/2 oz/¹/4 cup) dried apricots
90 g (3¹/4 oz/¹/2 cup) pitted dried dates
250 g (9 oz) instant couscous
55 g (2 oz/¹/4 cup) caster (superfine)
sugar
250 ml (9 fl oz/1 cup) boiling water
90 g (3¹/4 oz) unsalted butter, softened

TO SERVE
2 tablespoons caster (superfine) sugar
¹/2 teaspoon ground cinnamon
375 ml (13 fl oz/1¹/2 cups) hot milk

SERVES 4–6

Preheat the oven to 160°C (315°F/Gas 2–3). Spread the nuts on a baking tray and bake for 5 minutes, until light golden. Allow to cool, then roughly chop and place in a bowl. Slice the apricots into matchstick-sized pieces and quarter the dates lengthways. Add to the bowl and toss to combine.

Put the couscous and sugar in a large bowl and cover with the boiling water. Stir well, then add the butter and a pinch of salt. Stir until the butter melts. Cover with a tea towel and set aside for 10 minutes. Fluff with a fork, then toss half the fruit and nut mixture through.

To serve, pile the warm couscous in the centre of a platter. Arrange the remaining nut mixture around the base. Combine the sugar and cinnamon in a small bowl and serve separately for sprinkling. Pass around the hot milk for guests to help themselves.

PREPARATION TIME: 20 MINUTES + COOKING TIME: 5 MINUTES

GULAB JAMUN

100 g (3¹/2 oz/1 cup) milk powder
50 g (1³/4 oz/¹/2 cup) ground almonds
150 g (5¹/2 oz) plain (all-purpose) flour
1 teaspoon baking powder
¹/2 teaspoon ground cardamom
30 g (1 oz) butter, chopped
60 g (2¹/4 oz/¹/4 cup) plain yoghurt
oil, for deep-frying
220 g (7³/4 oz/1 cup) sugar
a few drops of rosewater

MAKES 35

Sift the dry ingredients into a large bowl and add the butter. Rub the butter into the flour with your fingertips until the mixture resembles fine breadcrumbs. Make a well, then add the yoghurt and 2–3 tablespoons of water. Mix with a flat-bladed knife to form a soft dough (alternatively, use a food processor). Shape the dough into small balls about the size of quail eggs, cover with a damp cloth and set aside.

Fill a heavy-based saucepan one-third full of oil and heat to 180°C (350°F), or until a cube of bread dropped into the oil turns golden brown in 15 seconds. Deep-fry the jamuns in several batches until deep brown. Do not cook them too quickly or the middle won't cook through. They should puff up a little. Drain in a sieve set over a bowl.

Put the sugar and 375 ml (13 fl oz/1¹/2 cups) water in a heavy-based saucepan and stir until the sugar has dissolved. Bring to the boil, reduce the heat and simmer for 5 minutes. Stir in the rosewater. Place the warm jamuns in a deep bowl and pour the syrup over them. Leave to soak and cool a little. Drain and serve warm, piled in a small bowl.

PREPARATION TIME: 20 MINUTES COOKING TIME: 25 MINUTES

Sweet couscous

PEACH CHARLOTTES WITH MELBA SAUCE

220 g (7¾ oz/1 cup) sugar
6 peaches, unpeeled
80 ml (2½ fl oz/⅓ cup) peach liqueur
2 loaves brioche
100 g (3½ oz) butter, melted
160 g (5½ oz/½ cup) apricot jam, warmed and sieved
raspberries, extra, to serve

MELBA SAUCE
300 g (10½ oz) fresh or thawed frozen raspberries
2 tablespoons icing (confectioners') sugar

SERVES 4

Preheat the oven to 180°C (350°F/Gas 4). Brush four 250 ml (9 fl oz/1 cup) ovenproof ramekins or dariole moulds with melted butter.

Put the sugar and 1 litre (35 fl oz/4 cups) water in a large heavy-based saucepan. Stir over medium heat until the sugar completely dissolves. Bring to the boil, then reduce the heat slightly and add the whole peaches. Simmer, covered, for 20 minutes. Drain and cool. Peel the skins and slice the flesh thickly. Place the peach slices in a bowl, sprinkle with the liqueur and set aside for 20 minutes.

Cut the brioche into 1 cm (½ inch) thick slices and remove the crusts. With a scone-cutter, cut out rounds to fit the tops and bases of each ramekin. Cut the remaining slices into 2 cm (¾ inch) wide fingers and trim to fit the height of the ramekins. Dip the first round into melted butter and place in the base of the ramekin. Dip the brioche fingers into the melted butter and press around the side of the ramekin, overlapping slightly. Line all the ramekins with the brioche in this manner.

Fill the lined ramekins evenly with peach slices and top each with the last round of brioche dipped in melted butter. Press to seal. Put the ramekins on a baking tray and bake for 20 minutes.

Meanwhile, make the melba sauce. Put the berries in a food processor and add the icing sugar (you may need a little more, depending on the sweetness of the berries). Process until smooth, then push the berries through a fine sieve.

Turn the peach charlottes out onto serving plates, brush with the warmed jam and pour some melba sauce alongside. Serve with extra berries if desired.

PREPARATION TIME: 30 MINUTES +   COOKING TIME: 40 MINUTES

NOTE: The peaches can be cooked, the ramekins lined with brioche and the sauce made up to 6 hours ahead. Refrigerate the charlottes, then fill and bake them close to serving time.

BERRY MERINGUE STACKS

2 egg whites
115 g (4 oz/^{1}/$_2$ cup) caster (superfine) sugar
250 g (9 oz) strawberries
150 g (5^1/$_2$ oz) blueberries
125 g (4^1/$_2$ oz) raspberries
1 tablespoon soft brown sugar
375 ml (13 fl oz/1^1/$_2$ cups) cream, whipped
icing (confectioners') sugar, to dust

SERVES 6

Preheat the oven to 150°C (300°F/Gas 2). Line baking trays with baking paper and mark out eighteen 9 cm (3^1/$_2$ inch) circles.

Using electric beaters, beat the egg whites in a clean, dry large bowl until soft peaks form. Gradually add the sugar, beating after each addition, until the mixture is thick and glossy. Spread 1 tablespoon of the mixture evenly over each of the circles to a thickness of 5 mm (1^1/$_4$ inches). Bake for 30–35 minutes, or until lightly golden, then turn the oven off and leave the meringues to cool completely in the oven.

Trim the strawberries and combine with the other berries in a large bowl. Sprinkle with the brown sugar, then cover and refrigerate for 20 minutes.

To assemble, using three meringue circles for each, place one on a plate, spread with cream and arrange some of the berries over the cream. Place another circle on top, spread with cream, top with more berries and then top with the third circle. Dust liberally with icing sugar. Repeat this with all the circles to make six individual stacks. Serve immediately.

PREPARATION TIME: 50 MINUTES   COOKING TIME: 35 MINUTES

MELON MEDLEY

^{1}/$_2$ rockmelon or any orange-fleshed melon
^{1}/$_2$ honeydew melon
^{1}/$_4$ watermelon
pulp from 2 passionfruit

SERVES 4

Cut the melons into bite-sized pieces or use a melon baller to scoop the flesh into balls. Chill, covered, for 30 minutes. Divide among serving bowls and drizzle with the passionfruit.

PREPARATION TIME: 10 MINUTES +   COOKING TIME: NIL

DEVIL'S FOOD CAKE

280 g (10 oz/1½ cups) soft brown sugar
40 g (1½ oz/⅓ cup) unsweetened cocoa powder
250 ml (9 fl oz/1 cup) milk
90 g (3¼ oz) dark chocolate, chopped
125 g (4½ oz) unsalted butter, softened
1 teaspoon natural vanilla extract
2 eggs, separated
185 g (6½ oz/1½ cups) plain (all-purpose) flour
1 teaspoon bicarbonate of soda (baking soda)

CHOCOLATE ICING
50 g (1¾ oz) dark chocolate, chopped
30 g (1 oz) unsalted butter
1 tablespoon icing (confectioners') sugar

FILLING
250 ml (9 fl oz/1 cup) whipping cream
1 tablespoon icing (confectioners') sugar
1 teaspoon natural vanilla extract

SERVES 8–10

Preheat the oven to 160°C (315°F/Gas 2–3). Lightly grease two deep 20 cm (8 inch) round cake tins and line the bases with baking paper. Combine a third of the brown sugar with the cocoa and milk in a small saucepan. Stir over low heat until the sugar and cocoa have dissolved. Remove from the heat and stir in the chocolate, stirring until melted. Cool.

Cream the remaining brown sugar with the butter in a small bowl with electric beaters until light and fluffy. Beat in the vanilla and egg yolks and the cooled chocolate mixture. Transfer to a large bowl and stir in the sifted flour and bicarbonate of soda.

Beat the egg whites in a clean, dry small bowl until soft peaks form. Fold into the chocolate mixture. Divide the mixture evenly between the tins. Bake for 35 minutes, or until a skewer inserted in the centre of the cakes comes out clean. Leave in the tins for 5 minutes before turning out onto a wire rack to cool.

To make the chocolate icing, put the chocolate and butter in a heatproof bowl. Place the bowl over a saucepan of simmering water, making sure it doesn't touch the water, and stir until the mixture is melted and smooth. Gradually add the sifted icing sugar and stir until smooth.

To make the filling, whip the cream, icing sugar and vanilla in a small bowl with electric beaters until stiff peaks form. Spread over one of the cold cakes, top with the second cake and spread with icing, over the top or top and sides.

PREPARATION TIME: 30 MINUTES   COOKING TIME: 45 MINUTES

ORANGE SORBET

10–12 oranges
90 g (3¼ oz/¾ cup) icing (confectioners') sugar
2 teaspoons lemon juice

SERVES 6

Cut the oranges in half and carefully squeeze out the juice, taking care not to damage the skins. Dissolve the icing sugar in the orange juice, add the lemon juice and pour into a metal freezer container. Cover the surface with baking paper and freeze for 1 hour.

Scrape the remaining flesh and membrane out of six of the orange halves, cover the six skin halves with plastic wrap and refrigerate.

After 1 hour, stir any frozen juice that has formed around the edge of the sorbet into the centre and return to the freezer. Repeat every hour, or until nearly frozen. Freeze overnight.

Divide the sorbet among the orange skins and freeze until ready to serve. This sorbet may seem very hard when it has frozen overnight but it will melt quickly, so work fast.

PREPARATION TIME: 20 MINUTES +   COOKING TIME: NIL

PASSIONFRUIT AND ORANGE SORBET

750 ml (26 fl oz/3 cups) orange juice
185 g (6½ oz/¾ cup) passionfruit pulp
115 g (4 oz/½ cup) caster (superfine) sugar
2 egg whites, lightly beaten

SERVES 4

Mix the orange juice, passionfruit pulp and sugar in a large bowl, stirring until the sugar dissolves. Pour into a metal freezer container and freeze until just firm around the edges. Do not allow to become too firm. Transfer to a bowl or food processor and beat with electric beaters or process in a food processor. Refreeze. Repeat this step twice more, adding the egg white the final time, with the beaters or motor running. Return the sorbet to the container, cover with baking paper and freeze for 3 hours, or until firm.

Alternatively, pour the mixture into an ice-cream machine and churn for about 30 minutes. Serve in glass dishes.

PREPARATION TIME: 20 MINUTES +   COOKING TIME: NIL

SEMOLINA AND NUT DIAMONDS

115 g (4 oz) unsalted butter, softened
115 g (4 oz/$\frac{1}{2}$ cup) caster (superfine) sugar
125 g (4$\frac{1}{2}$ oz/1 cup) semolina
110 g (3$\frac{3}{4}$ oz/1 cup) ground roasted hazelnuts
2 teaspoons baking powder
3 eggs, lightly beaten
1 tablespoon finely grated orange zest
2 tablespoons orange juice
whipped cream or honey-flavoured yoghurt, to serve

SYRUP
660 g (1 lb 7 oz/3 cups) sugar
4 cinnamon sticks
1 tablespoon thinly julienned orange zest
80 ml (2$\frac{1}{2}$ fl oz/$\frac{1}{3}$ cup) lemon juice
125 ml (4 fl oz/$\frac{1}{2}$ cup) orange blossom water

TOPPING
60 g (2$\frac{1}{4}$ oz/$\frac{1}{2}$ cup) slivered almonds
70 g (2$\frac{1}{2}$ oz/$\frac{1}{2}$ cup) roasted hazelnuts, roughly chopped

MAKES 12

Preheat the oven to 210°C (415°F/Gas 6–7). Lightly grease a 23 cm (9 inch) square baking tin and line the base with baking paper.

Cream the butter and sugar in a bowl until light and fluffy. Stir in the semolina, ground hazelnuts and baking powder. Add the eggs, orange zest and orange juice and fold through until well combined. Spoon into the tin, smooth the surface and bake for 20 minutes, or until golden and just set. Leave in the tin.

Meanwhile, to make the syrup, put the sugar, cinnamon sticks and 800 ml (28 fl oz) water in a saucepan over low heat and stir until the sugar has dissolved. Increase the heat and boil rapidly, without stirring, for 5 minutes. Pour into a heatproof bowl, then return half to the saucepan. Boil for 15–20 minutes, or until thickened and reduced to about 170 ml (5$\frac{1}{2}$ fl oz/$\frac{2}{3}$ cup). Stir in the julienned orange zest.

Add the lemon juice and orange blossom water to the syrup in the bowl and pour it over the cake in the tin. When absorbed, turn the cake out onto a large flat plate. Slice into four equal strips, then slice each strip diagonally into three diamond-shaped pieces. Discard the end scraps but keep the pieces touching together.

To make the topping, combine the almonds and hazelnuts and scatter over the cake. Pour the thickened syrup and julienned orange zest over the nuts and leave to stand for 30 minutes before serving. Using a cake slice, transfer the diamonds to individual plates and serve with whipped cream or honey-flavoured yoghurt.

PREPARATION TIME: 30 MINUTES +   COOKING TIME: 45 MINUTES

CRANACHAN

2 tablespoons oatmeal
250 ml (9 fl oz/1 cup) whipping cream
2 tablespoons honey
1 tablespoon whisky
500 g (1 lb 2 oz) raspberries or strawberries
2 tablespoons rolled (porridge) oats, toasted

SERVES 6

Put the oatmeal in a small frying pan. Stir over low heat for 5 minutes, or until lightly toasted. Remove from the heat and cool completely.

Using electric beaters, beat the cream in a small bowl until soft peaks form. Add the honey and whisky and beat until just combined. Fold the cooled, toasted oatmeal into the cream mixture with a metal spoon.

Layer the berries and cream into six tall dessert glasses, finishing with the cream. Refrigerate for 2 hours and serve sprinkled with toasted oats.

PREPARATION TIME: 30 MINUTES +   COOKING TIME: 10 MINUTES

NOTE: In Scotland, charms are placed into cranachan at Halloween, somewhat like the customary coins in English Christmas puddings.

CHOCOLATE WHISKY LOAF

250 g (9 oz/1^2/$_3$ cups) chopped dark chocolate
60 g (2^1/$_4$ oz) unsalted butter, softened
4 egg yolks
310 ml (10^3/$_4$ fl oz/1^1/$_4$ cups) whipping cream
2 teaspoons natural vanilla extract
2 tablespoons whisky
3 tablespoons unsweetened cocoa powder, to dust

SERVES 6

Line a 21 x 14 x 7 cm (8^1/$_4$ x 5^1/$_2$ x 2^3/$_4$ inch) loaf (bar) tin with plastic wrap. Put the chocolate in a heatproof bowl. Half-fill a saucepan with water and bring to the boil, then remove the pan from the heat. Sit the bowl over the pan, making sure the base of the bowl doesn't touch the water. Stir occasionally until the chocolate has melted. Allow to cool.

Beat the butter and egg yolks in a small bowl until thick and creamy, then beat in the cooled chocolate. Beat the cream and vanilla in another bowl until soft peaks form, then fold in the whisky. Using a metal spoon, fold the cream and chocolate mixtures together until just combined.

Pour the mixture into the prepared tin, cover the surface with plastic wrap and freeze for 2–3 hours or overnight, until firm. Remove from the freezer, unmould and carefully peel away the plastic wrap. Smooth the wrinkles on the surface of the loaf using a flat-bladed knife. Place on a serving plate and dust with cocoa. If not serving immediately, return to the freezer for up to 1 week. Cut into slices to serve.

PREPARATION TIME: 20 MINUTES +   COOKING TIME: 5 MINUTES

LEMON PASSIONFRUIT SYLLABUB WITH BERRIES

2 teaspoons finely grated lemon zest

80 ml (2½ fl oz/⅓ cup) lemon juice

115 g (4 oz/½ cup) caster (superfine) sugar

125 ml (4 fl oz/½ cup) dry white wine

8 passionfruit

500 ml (17 fl oz/2 cups) thick (double/heavy) cream

500 g (1 lb 2 oz) blueberries

500 g (1 lb 2 oz) raspberries

2 tablespoons icing (confectioners') sugar

500 g (1 lb 2 oz) strawberries, halved

icing (confectioners') sugar, extra, to dust

SERVES 8–10

Stir the lemon zest, lemon juice, sugar and wine together in a bowl and set aside for 10 minutes. Cut the passionfruit in half and push the pulp through a sieve to remove the seeds. Add half the passionfruit pulp to the lemon and wine mixture.

Beat the cream with electric beaters until soft peaks form. Gradually beat in the lemon and passionfruit syrup until all the syrup is added (the mixture will have the consistency of softly whipped cream). Stir in the remaining passionfruit, cover and refrigerate for 1 hour.

Combine the blueberries, raspberries and icing sugar and place in a 2.5 litre (87 fl oz/10 cup) serving bowl. Spoon the cream mixture over the top. Decorate with the strawberry halves, dust with extra icing sugar and serve immediately.

PREPARATION TIME: 40 MINUTES +   COOKING TIME: NIL

NOTE: This traditional British custard dessert was originally made by beating milk or cream with wine, sugar, lemon juice and possibly spices, the acid curdling and thickening the mixture. Some versions were based on cider while others were further fortified with brandy. A thinner version was made as a drink and served at festive occasions in special syllabub glasses.

CREOLE RICE FRITTERS

90 g (3¼ oz/¾ cup) plain (all-purpose) flour
115 g (4 oz/½ cup) caster (superfine) sugar
½ teaspoon freshly grated nutmeg
1 teaspoon ground cinnamon
1 x 8 g (¼ oz) sachet instant dry yeast
2 eggs, lightly beaten
370 g (13 oz/2 cups) well-cooked short-grain rice, lightly mashed
1 teaspoon natural vanilla extract
vegetable oil, for deep-frying
icing (confectioners') sugar, to sprinkle

MAKES ABOUT 24

Sift the flour into a bowl and add the sugar, nutmeg, cinnamon, yeast and a large pinch of salt. Combine well. Gradually stir in 80 ml (2½ fl oz/ ⅓ cup) very hot but not boiling water until you have a thick paste. Gradually beat in the eggs and continue beating until you have a smooth batter, then mix in the rice and vanilla until well combined. Cover and set aside to rise in a warm, draught-free place for about 20 minutes, or until doubled in size. Stir well, then rest again for a further 20 minutes.

Pour enough oil into a deep-fryer or deep heavy-based saucepan to fully cover the fritters. Heat the oil to 180°C (350°F), or until a piece of batter dropped into the oil browns in 15 seconds. Stir the batter again, then, working in batches, drop tablespoons of the mixture into the hot oil and cook, turning occasionally, for 2–3 minutes, or until the fritters are deep golden. Drain on paper towels, sprinkle with icing sugar and serve immediately. Serve with ice cream if desired.

PREPARATION TIME: 20 MINUTES +   COOKING TIME: 15 MINUTES

RICE PUDDING WITH BERRIES

220 g (7¾ oz/1 cup) short-grain rice
125 g (4½ oz/½ cup) plain yoghurt
300 ml (10½ fl oz) pouring cream
80 g (2¾ oz/⅓ cup) caster (superfine) sugar
1 teaspoon natural vanilla extract
250 g (9 oz) strawberries, hulled and halved
300 g (10½ oz) fresh or frozen blueberries
1 tablespoon caster (superfine) sugar, extra

SERVES 4–6

Put the rice, ½ teaspoon salt and 625 ml (21½ fl oz/2½ cups) water in a saucepan and bring to the boil over high heat, stirring once. Reduce the heat and simmer, covered, for 20 minutes, or until very soft and tender but still moist. Remove from the heat and leave for 5 minutes.

Put the yoghurt, cream, sugar and vanilla in a bowl and whisk together. Leave at room temperature, stirring occasionally to dissolve the sugar.

Toss the strawberries, blueberries and extra sugar together in a bowl. Cover and refrigerate until ready to serve.

Stir the hot rice into the cream mixture. Add more milk or cream if the mixture is too thick. Serve topped with the strawberries and blueberries.

PREPARATION TIME: 10 MINUTES   COOKING TIME: 25 MINUTES

INDEX

INDEX